Human Genetics

Other titles in the series:

Reproductive Technology:
Towards a Theology of Procreative Stewardship
by Brent Waters

Information Technology and Cyberspace:
Extra-connected Living
by David Pullinger

Human Genetics

Fabricating the Future

ROBERT SONG

THE
PILGRIM
PRESS
Cleveland

Published in North America by
The Pilgrim Press
700 Prospect Avenue East
Cleveland, Ohio 44115-1100
pilgrimpress.com

Originally published in 2002 by
Darton, Longman and Todd Ltd
1 Spencer Court
140–142 Wandsworth High Street
London SW18 4JJ

ISBN 0-8298-1482-5

06 05 04 03 02   5 4 3 2 1

A catalogue record for this book is available from the Library of Congress

Printed and bound in Great Britain

Contents

Contents

Acknowledgements

MY FIRST DEBTS OF GRATITUDE are owed to Audrey Elkington, whose postgraduate work on the theological ethics of genetics made me aware of the significance of the subject, and to Frank White, who gave me the idea of writing a book on it. Living and working in the North-East of England has brought many pleasures. Amongst them is that it has allowed me to benefit from events organised by the Policy, Ethics and Life Sciences Research Institute (PEALS), based at the International Centre for Life in Newcastle-upon-Tyne; I am particularly indebted to discussions at a reading group convened by its Director of Outreach, Tom Shakespeare.

I am also very grateful to the following, who read and commented on one or more chapters: David Clough, Jim Francis, Dave Leal, Pete Moore, Tom Shakespeare, and Michael Whong-Barr. Professor Judith Goodship of the Institute of Human Genetics, University of Newcastle, kindly read through the glossary. Katie Worrall of Darton, Longman and Todd has been a generous and patient editor; to her credit is also due for conceiving the idea for the Ethics and Theology series of which this book is a part.

Parts of Chapters Three and Five were first aired in a paper given at the Centre for Christianity and Culture, Regent's College, Oxford, to be published in a forthcoming book on theology and technology edited by Dave Leal.

To one person above all I owe more than I can easily say: my wife, Margaret Masson, to whom this book is dedicated, with love.

chapter one

Introduction

What are the prospects for human genetics? Why is there so much anxiety about its possible implications? This introductory chapter looks at the 'yuk factor' and the idea of 'playing God', and outlines the approach taken in the rest of the book.

IN AN ARTICLE IN *Science* discussing the origins and goals of the Human Genome Project, James D. Watson, the project's first director and the original co-discoverer of the double helix structure of the DNA molecule, predicted:

> A more important set of instruction books will never be found by human beings. When finally interpreted, the genetic messages encoded within our DNA molecules will provide the ultimate answers to the chemical under-pinnings of human existence.[1]

He went on to add that deciphering the human genome would contribute to our knowledge of 'how we function as healthy human beings', and in particular would help us to understand the role of genetic factors in disease.

The prospects opened up by genetic knowledge are indeed awesome. Many terrible human diseases attributable to genetic malfunction – such as cystic fibrosis, Huntington's disease, or Duchenne muscular dystrophy – may one day be treatable by direct genetic intervention. Many diseases or conditions in which genetic factors play a role alongside environmental factors – such as some forms of cancer or heart disease – could soon be treated more effectively through individually tailored targeting of drugs or through other therapies that are derived from our increasing genetic knowledge. Selection of embryos in order to avoid passing on 'bad genes' is already beginning to take place, as is research into gene therapy on embryos inside the womb. Although by comparison the clinical results to date are somewhat disappointing – no form of direct gene therapy is yet routine medical practice, for example – most scientists seem to agree that this is more a matter of time and effort than of intrinsic problems with the science itself.

The possibilities do not stop there, of course. Much attention is being focussed on genetic tests which can inform people whether they are likely to fall ill from a particular disorder. We are beginning to gain significantly more insight into the role of genes in human behaviour and other human attributes. Intelligence, sexuality, dispositions towards aggressiveness or nurturing, all may have an important genetic component, even if the relation of that component to environmental factors is complex and difficult to unravel. Elsewhere, genetic fingerprinting is assisting the police in their enquiries and is contributing to an increasing number of convictions. Historians and anthropologists will benefit from bioarchaeological information about migrations of peoples. And so on.

Despite these remarkable prospects, however, at least as much attention has been fixed on the potential dangers of the new genetic and biological technologies. Ever since the announcement that Dolly the sheep had been cloned by scientists in Edinburgh in 1997, the extension of the techniques to the cloning of human beings has been of huge international concern. Similarly, newspapers know that they will find a ready readership for articles about the possibility of designer babies chosen from catalogues to suit parental preferences, or of an uninsurable genetic underclass who cannot gain access to health or life cover because of their genetic status, or of the dangers of biotechnology companies using the patenting system to stake a claim on genes for which they appear to have found little clear practical application. And as a result of this it has been

easy for columnists, pressure group activists, pundits and professional worriers in general – not least the writers of ethics
books! – to talk about slippery slopes and a seemingly inevitable
descent towards genetically derived perdition.

It would be easy to dismiss these fears as irrational and based
on ignorance. Many of those who are strong champions of the
new genetics succumb to this temptation, perhaps in part
because of an understandable irritation at the lack of scientific
knowledge that often pervades people's attitudes on the subject
of genetics. Yet these concerns are not simply rooted in a naïve
rejection of science or antagonism towards it, as if the problem
could be solved by employing more professors of the public
understanding of science. Nor are they solely the product of a
'yuk factor', if by that phrase is meant a sheerly visceral reaction
which is closed to rational argument. Such analyses of popular
disquiet miss the point. What the optimists often lack is a
sufficiently sensitive appreciation of the underlying anxieties
which give rise to the alarmist headlines and predictions of
gloom – anxieties which may have rather more substance than
a mere instinctive and unscientific opposition to reason and
progress. Of course, the widely felt repugnance towards a
number of the new techniques may be partly a result of unwarranted prejudice and unexamined fear, and there are many
examples from history (for example, vaccinations, heart transplants, and, most recently, *in vitro* fertilisation techniques)
where initial gut feelings of antipathy have given way – rightly
or wrongly – to qualified or even total public acceptance.
However as biologist and philosopher Leon Kass has argued,
it could also in part be the surface expression of a deeper,
sedimented wisdom which is not so easy to put into words,
but which preserves some of our deepest moral intuitions. Its
superficial irrationality could mask a profound rationality
which it would be foolish to despise.[2]

How should we account for this public unease? One possibility is that such reactions are simply an expression of a fear
of the future which often accompanies technological developments. The terrors of the unknown inevitably haunt the

imagination, and religion in particular has too often reaped benefits by playing on them. But to reduce public technophobia with regard to genetics to this fails to explain why genetics is singled out for such concern, when many areas of scientific and technological advance do not attract the same degree of apprehension: most potential advances in medical treatments, for example, are greeted with acclaim.

It is surely closer to the mark to see such fears as based on concern about interfering with 'nature', particularly that part of nature which is the human body. It is no accident that the myth of Frankenstein plays such a large role in many people's instinctive reactions to the new biotechnologies: it potently articulates our desires and fears about our burgeoning capacity to manipulate human bodies by technological means. But, this being so, it would be foolish to imagine that the story of Frankenstein is simply an irrational fantasy which demonstrates the naïvety of those opposed to genetic research, and that we could just as easily tell another, more cheering story about scientific progress. The truth is that if Frankenstein and his monster had never existed, it would have been necessary to invent them. The fears expressed through the myth need to be understood and appreciated, not dismissed.[3]

Mary Shelley's story *Frankenstein* differs from earlier myths about the human creation of life, such as the golem of Jewish legend, in that for the first time life is created by the scientist's effort alone, without the invocation of God or some supernatural agency. And this suggests a second aspect of our fears about manipulating the body, namely that it is 'playing God'. The frequent resort to this language when discussing aspects of the new genetics might be regarded as evidence of a residual and essentially outdated religiosity. But it is at least as plausible to see it as one way of expressing an authentic recognition of human finitude, that whatever we are and whoever God is, we do at least know that we do not have the omnipotence or omniscience of a divine Creator. The power of technology to enable human beings to probe the depths of biological life itself, and then to manipulate it to advantage, seems to be trespassing on what is the prerogative of the Creator alone. Certainly, it is a power which no one could lightly take upon him or herself. If this intuition, or something like it, is in truth a significant element in the public reaction, then far from being discarded, it deserves to be treated with the highest seriousness.

Precisely because such fears have been such a central feature of the impact of genetic technologies on contemporary Western societies, any ethical approach to issues in human genetics which ignores them runs the danger of inappropriate abstraction. Too often philosophical and theological bioethics is written as if the limit of the moral task is to discern what are the correct principles to be applied in a particular situation, without any sense of the cultural expectations and technological dynamics which have brought particular techniques or procedures into existence, and which will powerfully contribute to their shaping in the future. Ethics needs to be embodied, and that involves an understanding not only of principle, but also of context. In the case of genetics, a major part of that context is what has been called the 'technological imperative', the drive to mastery of nature which serves significantly to structure our beliefs and actions, whether we are aware of it or not, whether we like it or not.

For this reason I have tried to do more than provide lists of arguments on each side of the particular moral issues raised by human genetics, even if many of these will also be covered in the course of the book. Rather, I have attempted to understand some of the fundamental causal factors – the attitudes, beliefs, and existential commitments, as well as the medical, scientific and commercial pressures – which have governed developments in modern medical genetics. It is primarily in relation to these underlying concerns that I pose some of the central questions raised by Christian theological ethics. Adopting such an approach enables us to recognise that the salient moral issues are common to many of the differing techniques connected with the new genetics: what unites them is greater than what divides them. It also helps to ease one of the besetting problems facing anyone who writes on the ethics of genetics, namely the awesome speed with which the technologies develop; as has been said, 'If it is in print, it is out of date!' The important question is to understand the underlying trends behind the presenting issues.

Chapter Two centres on an understanding of health and medicine within the Christian tradition, and how this might apply to the new genetics. Christianity has had a long-standing commitment to the practice of healing, rooted in its under-standing of God's salvation through Christ, and as a result has always been broadly receptive to modern Western scientific medicine. This should guide a significant part of its response to the Human Genome Project, and medical genetics more generally: too often those who are critical of aspects of it fail to give adequate recognition to the promise of new and more powerful clinical treatments which could, over decades, make a massive contribution to human health and well-being. These are in the early stages of development at the moment, but the prospects for medicine are unquestionably exciting. This is not to say that every related development has been uncontroversial, and in the second half of the chapter I consider three particular techniques – pre-implantation genetic diagnosis, reproductive cloning, and stem-cell research – which have been widely debated.

Genetic science, as we have just seen, is not associated in the public mind solely with potential medical benefits, and in Chapter Three I turn to consider the possibility of enhancement-related genetic engineering. The promise – or the threat – of designer babies is arguably a contemporary reprise of an older theme, that of the eugenic movement of the earlier part of the twentieth century. The history of this movement, massively influential in English-speaking countries as well as in Nazi Germany, is still too little known. Moreover, many maintain that it has re-emerged in the so-called 'new eugenics' of pre-natal testing and abortion, a claim which entails an investi-gation of the kind of pressures that lead people to resort to these procedures, and the views of disability which are implicit in them. Similar pressures, I suggest, may also lead to positive eugenic engineering. If such an outcome is to be rejected, the question has to be addressed of whether some distinction between therapy and enhancement can be established: a distinction, that is, between acceptable and unacceptable forms of genetic manipulation. And from a Christian perspective, that also requires an understanding of the theological issues at stake.

One of the most important themes for any Christian ethic is that of justice and human community. In Chapter Four I use this to explore three seemingly unrelated topics: behavioural genetics, the use of gene testing for insurance purposes, and gene patenting. The analysis of the differing contributions made by genes and environment to individual behaviour has made behavioural genetics one of the most controversial and politically sensitive of all issues raised by the new genetics. The first question it evokes for many concerns fears about genetic determinism, whether untangling the influence of genetics on behaviour might imply a denial of human liberty and responsibility. However, I argue that the deeper problem relates to its implications for justice. Whether in the discovery of an alleged 'gay gene' or in the purported connections between intelligence and race drawn by the authors of *The Bell Curve*, the real questions posed by the new genetic understanding are whether it reinforces discrimination or enables a new appreciation of human community. Similar issues are involved in the use of genetic information by insurers, and in the implicit question of whether genetic risks are burdens that should be borne by the individual or collectively by the community. The role of commercial interests over against the public good is also central to the discussion of gene patenting, as it is in thinking about genetics and global justice.

Chapter Five ties together a number of themes from the earlier chapters by exploring the background anxiety about runaway technology. Although many people are instinctively opposed to central parts of eugenic genetic engineering, they also believe that it is likely to happen, whatever their views. This sense of the inevitability of genetic engineering, as part of a broader 'necessity of technology', generates a constant feeling of bewilderment that our ethics are unable to keep pace with our technology. This is not adequately addressed by ethical approaches which see the task of ethics as simply that of applying principles or methods to particular genetic techniques, as if concluding that they were wrong would make them go away. Rather, what is needed is a grasp of the much longer-term cultural aspirations which have given rise to these techniques, an understanding which I frame in terms of the Baconian project of eliminating suffering and expanding the realm of human choice. In response to this there is a need for an alternative vision of society and the human good, one which is not driven by the compulsions and hectoring necessities that generate the technological imperative. It is not wrong for us to hope that the church might form the embodiment of such a vision. This would be a matter not so much of its making the correct public pronouncements, valuable though those may be, but of discovering those ways of living together that would truly express the nature of created human beings freed to love God.

Inevitably it is not possible to address all the moral issues raised by the new genetics in a short book such as this. I have made no effort to address questions about confidentiality of genetic test results in a clinical context, for example, or about the use of genetic information by current or future employers, and I make only the briefest of references to germ-line gene therapy. I have also categorically left out of consideration all matters to do with plant or animal genetics, such as the morality of genetically modified crops, xenotransplantation or animal genetic experimentation. References for all of these are provided in the Select Annotated Bibliography for those who wish to pursue them.

chapter two

Health, Medicine and the New Genetics

This chapter sets the Human Genome Project in the context of the Christian tradition's understanding of health and medicine, and describes the possible clinical benefits of the new genetics. It also discusses some controversial medical outcomes of genetic research:

- pre-implantation genetic diagnosis (PGD)
- reproductive cloning
- stem-cell research.

These topics also require a separate discussion of the status of the embryo.

IN THINKING ABOUT human genetics from a theological perspective, I want to start from a theological understanding of the nature of health and medicine. This affirms the Christian commitment to healing and care for those who are sick, but also sets this commitment within a wider Christian witness to the cosmic nature of human salvation. It allows a proper role for technological medicine in the Christian work of care for the sick, but it also ensures that such medicine does not attempt to exceed its subordinate role in relation to God's overarching work of redemption. In this chapter I will focus on the therapeutic role of genetic medicine. This will involve a discussion of the Human Genome Project and its potential medical benefits. These should not be played down, I shall suggest: too often those who are critical of aspects, even central aspects, of developments in genetics can give the impression of being opposed to genetic science root and branch. But we shall also consider some more controversial medical outcomes connected with genetics: pre-implantation genetic diagnosis, human reproductive cloning, and stem-cell research.

Health and medicine in Christian perspective

For Christians physical healing has always been viewed in the light of salvation in Jesus Christ.[1] While a commitment to healing has been a central feature of the ministry of the church from New Testament times onwards, this has always been subordinated to an understanding of humanity as fallen but redeemed in Christ. Sickness and suffering have been seen not as evils which are meaningless in themselves, but rather as reminders of the nature of human beings as lapsed from their original created goodness. As George Khushf puts it, they relate 'to the deeper spiritual predicament of sin in the same way that symptoms relate to a disease'.[2] Suffering is in fact a kind of revelation of the situation of human beings in general. Just as the fall has resulted in our alienation from ourselves, from each other, and from God, so pain may cause us to disassociate ourselves from the bits of our bodies that are suffering, turning us in on ourselves, and isolating us from others and from any sense of the presence of God. Sometimes an encounter with illness can be an intense, unvarnished experience of the underlying malaise of the human situation.

But it is not only the fall that can be symbolised in our immediate human experience. Redemption likewise can be made manifest to us. In the Christian ministry of healing, works of healing are symbols of salvation in Christ, both in the sense that they indicate what salvation is like, and in that they embody some of its reality. It is this close relation between the two which explains why salvation and healing are so intimately linked in the New Testament, in a way that can seem confused to the modern mind. Jesus goes throughout Galilee both preaching the Gospel and healing the sick (Matt. 4:23); it is no accident that the two are found together in many places in the Gospels. Thus one of the principal New Testament words for salvation, *sôteria*, is also used to mean healing, and on a number of occasions – such as the healing of the paralytic (Mark 2:1–12) – Jesus' power to forgive sins is related to his pronouncement of healing. Not only sickness, but evil and death also are results of the fall: in the ministry of Jesus they are all confronted, through miracles of healing, the casting out of demons and the raising of the dead. Indeed, such works of Jesus are supreme indicators of the presence of the Kingdom: 'if it is by the finger of God that I cast out the demons, then the kingdom of God has come upon you' (Luke 11:20).

Jesus' works of healing make immediate to human experience the presence of the Kingdom. They express in tangible form the new underlying reality that is beginning to break in on the old order of sin and death. But healing is not an activity isolated from other dimensions of human existence. In the Nazareth manifesto described in Luke 4:16–21, recovery of sight for the blind is one of a series of promises which includes good news to the poor, release to the captives, and freedom to the oppressed, all of them signs of the Jubilee year of the Lord's favour. Healing is inseparable from the restoration of right relationships and the establishment of justice. Together they point to and participate in *shalom*, the word used to describe the ancient Jewish vision of a time of righteousness, wholeness, harmony, and peace. In such a time, in the new heaven and new earth, death and mourning and crying and pain will be no more (Rev. 21:3–4; cf. Isa. 65:17–25).

Unsurprisingly, then, the practice of healing has been central to the church's mission. After Pentecost, one of the first stories told of the infant church is of healing in the name of Christ (Acts 3:1–10). Amongst the spiritual gifts listed in 1 Corinthians are gifts of healing by the Holy Spirit (1 Cor. 12:9, 28). Elsewhere those who are sick are urged to call for the elders of the church, who will pray over them, anointing them with oil in the name of the Lord; such healing is closely connected with the forgiveness of sins (Jas. 5:13–16). Throughout Christian history, the church has been involved with the foundation of hospitals and hospices, as means of hospitality to those who are ill and in need of care. Whether through the laying on of hands and anointing with oil, or with the assistance of modern Western scientific medicine, caring for the sick has been seen as one of the requirements of Christian faithfulness (cf. Matt. 25:36).

Yet the removal of suffering has never been seen as the supreme goal in itself. Precisely because it is part of a larger story about the redemption of creation, Christians have always believed that there may be things more valuable in this transient life than a mere absence of pain. Afflicted by an unidentified thorn in the flesh, the apostle Paul cries out for relief, but is told by the Lord that his weakness is an opportunity to know the power of Christ dwelling in him: 'My grace is sufficient for you' (2 Cor. 12:7–10). In Gethsemane Jesus prays that the cup of suffering will be removed from him, but wrestles with obedience to the will of God: 'yet not my will be done, but thine' (Mark 14:36). Sharing in Christ's sufferings and becoming like him in his death is part of knowing Christ and the power of his resurrection (Phil. 3:10). Suffering can produce endurance, which in turn produces character and then hope (Rom. 5:3–5). The scope for growing in depth of knowledge of God through suffering means that suffering cannot be regarded as in principle meaningless, something which could rob life of all significance.

Of course, there are profound dangers in such a view of suffering: the idea that all things work together for good for those who love God (Rom. 8:28) may too easily degenerate into a glib denial of the fathomless sense of absurdity that suffering can sometimes open up. But it remains the case that in Christian faith it is the possibility of meaning, however distant at times it may seem, which sets the context for interpreting suffering; it is not the reality of suffering which renders pointless the search for meaning.

This placing of questions of suffering and healing in the context of the cosmic drama of redemption gives Christian views of health and medicine their characteristic twofold nature. It has generated on the one hand a deep commitment to healing and caring for people in their need, and on the other a willingness to accept suffering and to look for good and hints of meaning in it. Together with the symbolic nature of both illness and healing, pointing towards the greater story of sin and redemption, this twofold approach powerfully distinguishes Christian views from contemporary secular ones. Modern Western culture tends towards an idolisation of health, such that serious illness becomes perhaps the worst thing that can happen to one, short of death. Health is regarded as the normal state of being, and disease or disability as an abnormal deviation. For Christians, however, illness is a reminder of the true situation of human beings: it 'discloses a deep brokenness that is there already, and not brought about for the first time by the sickness'.[3] For this reason it is not something which is intrinsically senseless, to which the only meaningful response is rejection and escape. While it is never to be regarded as good – it points, after all, to the fall – there are good things which may arise in and from it.

The role of healing is also to be placed in its wider, cosmic context. Care of the sick, grounded in the compassionate sharing of the sufferer's pain and seeking ways of alleviating and perhaps curing it, is a witness to God's work of redemption in Jesus Christ. However, any form of medicine which implicitly denies this context runs the danger of itself becoming a surrogate kind of salvation. In previous times, that quasi-salvific role has often been taken by certain kinds of magic. In the modern world it has more typically been taken by technological medicine. While medicine assisted by technological advance might be capable of being subordinated to a humbler and more honest position, more often scientific progress has come to be seen as the saviour of the world. Nowhere has that role been more potent than in modern technological medicine.

This Christian perspective on health and medicine sets the

context for our thinking about recent scientific and technological developments in genetics. On the one hand, it requires
a strong acknowledgement of the role that they can play in the
work of healing. Too often those who are critical of aspects of
such developments, or fearful of their possible consequences,
give the impression that there is nothing of value in them. I
shall argue to the contrary, that they are capable of making
enormous contributions to medicine, which should not be mini-
mised. While, of course, these technological advances are not
without danger – not even their most ardent defenders would
claim that they are – the promise, over time, which they hold
out should not be denied. On the other hand, as we shall see
later, such advances in understanding human genetics also have
a massive capacity for contributing to the ideas that disease is
simply an aberration and suffering intrinsically pointless, that
healing of the body is entirely separable from any questions of
justice or right relationship, and that everything needful for
human flourishing can be found through scientific progress.

For the moment, however, it is to the first of these, the medical
promise of recent developments in scientific understanding,
that we shall turn.

The Human Genome Project

The principal research effort in human genetics in the last
decade has centred on the Human Genome Project (HGP).
While plenty of other research on the human genome was
taking place before it was launched and has continued to do
so since, it is this international, multi-million-pound project
which has rightly had the highest profile. Begun in 1990 after
several years of discussion, the HGP was a long-term upshot
of the discovery of the molecular structure of DNA by James
Watson and Francis Crick in 1953. It had long been clear that
if the genetic structure of human beings was to be properly
understood, with all the implications this would have for
understanding the functioning of the human organism and

for unravelling the genetic contribution to disease, the DNA code for the whole human genome would have to be deciphered. This in turn would require sequencing the entire three billion base pairs of the genome and identifying all the genes it contains, a number which has come down on the most recent estimates to about 30,000.

The project has been principally financed by the US government and the British medical charity, the Wellcome Trust, and research has taken place in several countries in addition to Britain and the US. Initial efforts were devoted to establishing a map of genetic markers, identifiable sequences of six or eight letters of the code contained within the chromosomes which could be used as initial signposts for subsequent, more detailed work. Simultaneous projects also aimed at determining the entire genetic sequences of simpler and more manageable organisms such as nematode worms, bacteria and fruit flies. Attention then turned to sequencing the human genome itself. Here progress was made much more quickly and cheaply than had been initially expected, not least because the project of sequencing was turned into a race by the dramatic announcement in 1998 by Celera Genomics, a private biotechnology corporation, that it would finish a first draft years earlier than the HGP. In December 1999 the sequencing of chromosome 22 was announced, the first chromosome to be completed. On 26 June 2000 a complete 'working draft' of the genome was announced: Bill Clinton declared in a White House press conference that it was 'the most wondrous map ever produced by mankind', while in a joint announcement Tony Blair described it as 'a breakthrough that opens the way for massive advancement in the treatment of cancer and hereditary diseases, and that is only the beginning'.

The work of sequencing the genome is certainly only a beginning. After the rough draft comes filling in the gaps and checking the sequence for accuracy. Then the task, already well under way, will need to be carried through of identifying all the human genes within the sequence and determining their function. A Human Genome Diversity Project has been established which aims to study the variation in the genome between different populations; this requires collecting DNA samples from around the world. There is also a fledgling Human Proteome Project, which is investigating possibilities of mapping all the proteins in the body (collectively known as the human proteome) and their interactions. The 'biological revolution' has still a long way to go.

What are the potential medical benefits of the Human Genome Project and other related advances in genetic technology? Clearly, finding genes associated with genetic disorders will be a major advance. More detailed genetic maps have already aided the discovery of genes associated with myotonic dystrophy, fragile-X syndrome, neurofibromatosis, inherited colon cancer, Alzheimer's disease, and familial breast cancer, amongst many others. Disorders due to single changes in single base pairs (known as single nucleotide polymorphisms, SNPs), will over time be more easily located. Diagnostic tests will be made more accurate, making possible earlier and more effective treatment of disease. Predictions about the future course of a disease will be more precise, allowing doctors to tell, for example, how aggressively a particular cancer will advance. Beyond that there is in general the promise of a profound change in the nature of medicine, concerned less with the treatment of symptoms and more with the fundamental causes of disease.

Amongst the first medical benefits that will reach the public will probably be personalised medicine. Pharmacogenomics (or pharmacogenetics, as it is also called) involves using genetic knowledge to tailor drugs for individual patients. Many drugs have low response rates: that is, although they may be effective for a large number of patients, they may also be ineffective or even positively harmful for others. Interferons, for example, which are used as anti-viral and anti-cancer treatments, are ineffective for about 25 per cent of patients (indeed for nearly 70 per cent, according to some studies). The reason for low response rates is not clear. While general health, age, environment, diet, other medications, and so on, no doubt play a part, many researchers believe that the single most important reason is genetic. If genetic links for different responses can be identified, it would allow for drugs to be targeted more accurately, not 'one-size-fits-all' as with current drugs, but tailor-made to improve response rates for different genetic types. This would also ensure that life-threatening side-effects are avoided. Currently up to a third of drugs fail to pass phase 3 trials, which include testing for serious side-effects; if 3 patients in 1000 die from adverse reactions, the drug on trial will not be marketed, to the loss of the vast majority who might have benefited. But if a genetic cause for the side-effect could be established, it would mean that those affected would not be prescribed the drug. This in turn would reduce the number of expensive failures at phase 3 trials, making drugs cheaper to develop and quicker to be approved, with consequent gains in health and health-care budgets. Advances in pharmacogenomics should also reduce the number of drugs patients have to try before finding an effective therapy and the length of time patients spend on particular medications, as well as increasing the range of possible drug targets and improving accuracy of drug dosages. Indeed, as many drugs come to be marketed together with DNA 'chips' that will quickly check thousands of gene locations for likely responses, it may even mean that some drugs, which were previously banned because of severe adverse reactions in a small percentage of cases, become available again.

The most discussed area of advance, which is not likely to come to fruition so soon, is in the area of gene therapy. Classical gene therapy turns on an idea which is conceptually easy to grasp, namely that a gene related to a disorder be removed and replaced by a version of the gene which is not 'defective'. In consequence, the gene would start expressing proteins which did not give rise to the disorder, and cure would have been effected at the level of the underlying genetic cause, not just the symptoms. In principle gene therapy could be targeted at two different kinds of cell: bodily tissues or organs such as lungs, liver or skin (known as somatic-cell gene therapy); or egg or sperm cells or embryos at a very early stage of development (known as germ-line therapy). The latter would affect not only every cell in the recipient, but would pass on changes to future generations as well. The former, however, would change the genome of the recipient alone, and would probably be limited to particular parts of the body (though there is some possibility that some forms of somatic-cell gene therapy might give rise to changes that would be passed on down the germ-line as well by accidentally affecting cells in the ovaries or testes).

In practice, however, gene therapy is firmly in its infancy. No germ-line therapy has yet been attempted in humans. Somatic-cell therapy is still primarily experimental: while the first officially approved procedure was undertaken in 1990, for a four-year-old girl with severe combined immune deficiency (SCID), clinical trials on human beings remain in the research stages. The practice of *gene surgery* or gene replacement, which is the process described above, requires a series of technological breakthroughs which have yet to take place. To date, gene therapy has instead relied on techniques of *gene addition*. The most common form of this has taken advantage of the abilities of certain kinds of viruses, known as retroviruses, to penetrate cells and insert their own DNA into the DNA in the cell nucleus. Scientists replace some of the viral DNA with a strand of DNA which they wish to insert into the host cell, and use the virus as a vehicle (known as a vector) to deliver the new genetic material to the target cells. But this has faced serious problems. Enough therapeutic genes have to be introduced into the host tissue to make a difference. The body has to be persuaded to adopt the genes without setting off a dangerous immune response (in 1999 Jesse Gelsinger, a volunteer in a gene therapy experiment at the University of Pennsylvania, died as a result of these side-effects). The genes also have to be inserted at a place in the host DNA which is not entirely random and does not interrupt important functioning sequences. As a result, although these and other problems are being addressed, the prospect of safe and effective gene therapies is still a way off.

Other applications and potential benefits of the new genetic knowledge are announced virtually daily. A combination therapy of chemotherapy and a genetically modified virus has shown promising results in shrinking head and neck cancers. Drugs have been produced which prevent RNA generating harmful proteins, and some have made it to the market to combat breast cancer, for example. Human genes are being spliced into bacterial cells, which are then grown in culture and used to manufacture therapeutic proteins which can be injected into the body as a conventional drug. And so on.

Some moral considerations

These advances are genuinely thrilling. They open up the possibilities of treatments and even cures which by today's standards are rightly regarded as extraordinarily powerful. The first signs of major new therapeutic tools are evident in fields which have seen relatively little major advance in recent times – cancer treatment, for example, which for a long time has largely stagnated around the three approaches of surgery, radiotherapy, and chemotherapy. To be sure, the promise of the new genetics, and the speed with which it will be able to provide safe and effective clinical results, has often been exaggerated, not least by scientists seeking research funding. However, even shorn of the hyperbole, the potential remains highly impressive.

But how should we evaluate them morally? Inevitably new powers always bring new dangers, and it is always possible that new kinds of moral problem will be thrown up which were not apparent when projects were first embarked on. Nevertheless, in my view most of these therapies do not raise any more – or any fewer – moral issues than are already raised by treatments which are already rightly accepted for use. With the exception of germ-line gene therapy, which I shall mention later, the questions prompted by these developments are those which are faced by all other proposed procedures.

Such questions would include, first, the safety of the proposed procedure. All new drugs and treatments must quite properly undergo rigorous testing for potential toxicity and adverse reactions, in which unwanted side-effects are proportionate to the expected benefits. Second, they should not be tested on anyone for experimental or research purposes, or used on anyone for therapeutic purposes, without the informed consent of that person. Third, procedures which are undertaken for research purposes must be reasonably expected to contribute to knowledge, while therapies which are made routinely available to the public must be of proven value. These kinds of requirements, whether or not they are expressed in exactly these terms, are at least widely recognised, even if – alarmingly – they are not always adhered to. I will not say more about them here.

But there are a further range of questions which deserve as much attention, and which should also be asked of all new developments, whether genetically related or not. For example, how would these affect the balance of power between rich countries and poor countries? Is money being spent on the diseases of the rich rather than those of the world's poor? Should money be spent on hi-tech cures, rather than on cheaper preventative medicine? What about animal experimentation? To what extent is it right that drugs should be tested on animals before they are transferred to human beings? Some of these questions will be addressed in subsequent chapters of this book.

Because of such uncertainties, there could never be a blanket approval of advances such as those described above. Moreover, there may be moral questions which apply to some of them but do not apply to others: would it be fair, for example, if someone apparently genetically unsuited to benefit from a pharmacogenetic product was denied the possibility of even trying it? Despite all such potential problems, however, there is at least a strong prima facie case for thinking that no more moral scruples should attend such genetically based therapies than already obtain in the case of other treatments. In these general terms, therefore, it might be possible for Christians to make use of such advances as part of a medical care which witnesses to the Kingdom of Christ.

This is not the case for all developments in the field of human genetics, however, and I now wish to turn to some which are considerably less straightforward. There are three which I am going to look at in some detail – pre-implantation genetic diagnosis, cloning for children, and stem-cell research – though what I shall have to say will also apply to germ-line gene therapy as well. All of these, particularly the two connected with cloning techniques, have raised considerable public debate, if not alarm, and the controversies surrounding them as yet show no signs of settling. I will address in turn the questions they raise, though I leave until the end one central question raised by them all, namely the status of the embryo.

Pre-implantation genetic diagnosis

Pre-implantation genetic diagnosis (PGD) is a technique that represents a culmination of developments in reproductive and genetic technologies. It is a procedure whereby embryos created outside the body can be screened for particular genetic defects before being implanted in the womb. Its principal use to date has been to assist those who wish to avoid passing on a dele-terious gene to their children, either by directly testing for a particular genetic disorder or by establishing the sex of an embryo (in cases where the disorder is sex-linked). The process requires creating an embryo outside the body through *in vitro* fertilisation. About two to three days after fertilisation, when the embryo consists of around six to ten cells, one or two cells are removed from the embryo, a process which appears to be compatible with the continuing development of the embryo. The genetic material in these cells is then examined, at the chromosomal level if it is a matter of establishing the sex for X-linked disorders or identifying chromosomal abnormalities, or at the level of the DNA sequence if it is (say) a single gene defect.

The most common uses for PGD worldwide are sexing embryos to avoid X-linked disorders and testing for abnormal numbers of chromosomes (as found in, for example, Down's syndrome, which is caused by having three chromosome 21s). For single-gene defects, cystic fibrosis is the most common disorder tested for, though an increasing number of other disorders are also being included as reliable tests become available: Tay-Sachs disease, Duchenne muscular dystrophy, Lesch Nyhan syndrome, and Marfan syndrome, amongst others.

PGD is not very widely used, at least currently. It was first successfully used in 1990, but even by 2000 there were only about 30 PGD cycles a year being undertaken in the UK (compared with about 30,000 IVF cycles and several hundreds of thousands of amniocentesis tests). This is in good part because with current technologies the success rate is simply not high enough: IVF success rates in the UK (i.e. IVF treatments leading to live births) currently average 17 per cent per cycle, and PGD rates are probably lower than IVF as a whole. PGD involves all the physical unpleasantness of IVF, which is largely a result of the powerful hormonal drugs required to stimulate hyperovulation, as well as its emotional uncertainty. And it is a lot more expensive, with almost all of the expense typically having to be met by the patients themselves.

This is not to suggest that PGD may not grow considerably. One of its chief attractions for many is that it avoids the physical and emotional stress associated with prenatal testing and abortion. Patients who use it know that they will not need to think about having an abortion, at least for the disorders for which the fetus was tested. But if PGD could be done with an easier and less problematic source of eggs, much of the trauma associated with it would disappear. Such a possibility is raised by current work on *in vitro* maturation of eggs; while this is still a long way from clinical application, it would allow a woman in her late teens to have a small part of an ovary removed and frozen, and eggs from it artificially matured when she was ready to have children.[4] Although PGD is small now, over some decades it could grow to become a significantly more important phenomenon.

There are a variety of other reasons why people are attracted to pre-implantation genetic diagnosis. Not only does it remove the element of risk where couples know that both are carriers of the same deleterious recessive gene, or that one has an autosomal dominant genetic disorder, so that a pregnancy can proceed without the wearing anxiety that a child may be affected. This also could be extended to not implanting carrier embryos; even if the child only had carrier status and would not develop a particular recessive disorder, it would never have to face the same potential agonising decision as the parents have had to. In cases where couples had suffered repeated miscarriages, it also could allow people to have the chance of having a child who might not have done otherwise: whereas IVF can select embryos that have the greatest chance of implanting and developing to term, PGD could also pinpoint possible genetic links. And for those who find abortion morally questionable on the grounds that it violates the personhood of the fetus, but do not regard the pre-implantation embryo as a person, selection of embryos at a pre-implantation stage might prove a more acceptable alternative.

On the other hand, there are also morally troubling aspects to pre-implantation diagnosis. In terms of safety, we are not yet fully sure of the long-term effects of the procedures on children born by them. Certainly there are no apparent signs of problems, and IVF has been performed now for over two decades without any obvious long-term side-effects; but on the other hand it is as yet unknown whether removing a cell or two from an early embryo is an additional risk factor.

Rather more important is a general question about our perceptions of disability. There is nothing wrong in making every effort to ensure that a healthy child is born, so long as this does not involve immoral means; and no good will ever come from heaping guilt on anxious would-be parents whose lives have been shattered by discovery of their genetic status. But this should not prevent us from also asking the question whether as a society we are locked into a cultural pattern of denial. PGD is too easily implicated in a mentality which avoids the issues of how we, both as a society and as individuals, come to terms with disability and the stigma attached to people with disabilities. As PGD becomes more readily available and clinically less problematic, it is not improbable that subtle pressure will grow on people with certain disorders to use it. That pressure would be as much internally generated as it would be social, medical or economic. Indeed it may become increasingly unacceptable to decide to give birth to a child who is known to have a particular disease; this process may be accelerated by the availability of PGD, since there currently remains a lot of understanding and sympathy for those women who cannot find it in them to abort an affected child. In other words, preimplantation genetic diagnosis is in danger of lending itself to a creeping, systematic bias against the birth of disabled children.

There are clear connections between this and the dominant mentality of consumerism. A consumer culture is not merely one which is wealthy and able to devote a lot of its resources to purchasing consumer goods. It is also a culture which turns the world into goods to be consumed: that is, it turns things which were previously regarded as beyond the reach of the money economy into things which can be bought and sold. In doing so it objectifies them, turning them into property and subjecting them to criteria of selection and quality control. Moreover, as a direct correlation, it also turns people into consumers – that is, those who relate to the world as possessing subjects over against possessed objects, who find fulfilment increasingly in ownership of and mastery over the world, and decreasingly in commitment to certain kinds of relationships and development of certain kinds of virtues.

Such a mentality is bad enough in many other areas of life, but it is disastrous when it starts encroaching on our attitudes to children. Instead of being accepted for themselves with an unconditional love that is willing to embrace them, whatever their capacities, there is a real risk that love becomes conditional on their meeting certain performance standards. Of course parents always run the danger of making their affection conditional through having unrealistic or over-demanding expectations of their children, and no doubt throughout history practical necessity has frequently led to a certain level of self-regard in having children. But the additional problem here is that the culture as a whole compounds such attitudes with a mind-set of commodification. It is this concern about the implicit drift towards treating children as objects, capable of being manufactured (extremely crudely at first, no doubt, but with increasing sophistication over time), which has always lain behind much of the church's suspicions of artificial reproductive technologies. As one writer has put it, 'If the baby is born and fails to meet expectations, will it be sent back to the factory? Will the parents ask for a refund? a discount?'[5] Of course, PGD is not by itself single-handedly bringing about such a wholesale commodifying mentality towards children: it is part of a much broader cultural trend. But when clinics face the possibility of being sued if they happen to make a mistake in their diagnosis, as will no doubt happen sooner or later, the parallels will become uncomfortably close.

None of these points should be taken to imply that those who have availed themselves of PGD and other similar techniques that forestall the birth of an affected child are individually prejudiced against people with disabilities. General considerations such as these are far too broad to deal with the complexity of personal circumstances in which individual people face such questions. But equally it would be irresponsible not to take such things into account, if we are serious about looking at the long-term implications of these developments. I will have much more to say about these broader cultural shifts in the next chapter when we discuss the 'new eugenics', after we have considered the genetic technologies connected with cloning.

Human cloning

All the anguished debates about human cloning that have taken place in the past few years across the world were ignited by a single event: the announcement on 24 February 1997 that scientists at the Roslin Institute in Edinburgh had successfully cloned an adult Finn Dorset sheep. While human cloning had previously received some moral discussion, particularly during the late 1960s, the state of the science had meant that this was always treated as a hypothetical extrapolation of technological trends rather than an immediate scientific reality. As the first successful attempt to create an adult clone of an adult mammal, however, Dolly brought much closer the vista of human cloning. The idea of cloning is of course freighted with deep cultural resonances, conjuring up futuristic images of a Brave New World of crushed individuality, cloned Hitlers and massed ranks of mindless automata. Such fears are especially potent in a society that prides itself on its individualism. Consequently it was not surprising that within days of the announcement President Clinton had ordered the National Bioethics Advisory Commission to produce a report within ninety days on the ethics of human cloning. Nor perhaps is it surprising that newspapers have continued to report a trickle of scientists who intend to offer a cloning service to anyone willing to pay.

The reality of the science is much more prosaic, needless to say. There are two methods which have been used to create genetically identical animals. Embryo splitting involves dividing embryos at an early stage so that two genetically identical embryos are formed; this is an artificial rendering of the natural process which gives rise to identical twins. Cloning itself, however, is more complex. Sometimes known as somatic cell nuclear transfer (SCNT) or cell nucleus replacement (CNR), it requires some version of the following process: taking the genetic material from the cell of an already existing individual, inserting it into an unfertilised egg from which the nucleus has been removed, and then activating the newly fertilised egg so that it starts dividing. The technique had eluded biologists for years, and Ian Wilmut succeeded where many had given up trying. Even then it was not immediately successful: the process of producing Dolly required cloning 277 sheep eggs in order to make one live birth possible.

After the initial furore over cloning had died down, it emerged that there were two different kinds of uses to which cloning might be put. These were (at least initially) described by the UK Human Genetics Advisory Commission as 'reproductive cloning' and 'therapeutic cloning'.[6] The first referred to the use of cloning techniques in order to create new human beings. The second referred to uses of them which would not require the implantation of cloned embryos in the womb; the most prominent of these has been in relation to stem-cell research. Although they both involve cloning techniques, the two raise almost entirely different sets of issues, and for this reason I shall treat them separately.

Reproductive cloning

Of the two, reproductive cloning is closer to what we naturally think of when we hear the phrase 'human cloning'. However, the situations for which it has realistically been proposed, questionable though they may be, are still far from the fevered alarmism of science fiction. They are rather part of the real world of contemporary reproductive technologies. Amongst the uses to which it might be put, for example, is to provide a last chance of children for couples for whom no other form of fertility treatment has worked. A cell would be taken from one or other of the couple, and its DNA inserted into an egg from the woman (or from another woman), and the egg, once activated, transferred into her uterus (or another woman's). Another possibility is that cloning would provide a chance for gay or (more obviously) lesbian couples to have children genetically related to at least one of them, an option which was initially received with enthusiasm by some gay and lesbian groups ('My twin has the right to be born', as one activist pronounced).[7] Cloning might also provide a means for single women to have children, if they were not in a relationship with someone whom they wanted to have as father of their child and did not wish the genetic risk of using unknown donor sperm. Others have seen cloning as a solution in cases where a compatible organ donor was needed: for example, if a bone marrow transplant was needed for a child suffering from leukaemia and nobody else could provide matching tissue, a cloned sibling could be a life-saver. Still others might look to cloning to replace a dead sibling who had been killed in an accident.

Many, perhaps all, of these cases could be justified by appeal to the language of the 'right to reproductive freedom'. In its most expansive form this alleged right is claimed to imply that individuals have a right to have children in any way they wish, in conjunction with anyone else they choose, using any artificial reproductive technologies that are available. The principal limits on such a freedom are safety, that nobody should be harmed, and consent, that nobody should be coerced. In the case of cloning, the parental right to have children in any way technologically open to them would create a strong presumption in favour of this approach to reproduction. Whether it could be rebutted would turn in good part on what kind of harms a cloned child might experience, and whether a child could be regarded as a consenting partner to these proceedings.

There are, of course, serious harms to a child that might arise from its being cloned. In terms of safety, for example, the failure rate experienced by the Roslin team would be entirely unacceptable in any efforts to clone human beings. Even if the techniques were improved, as is currently happening in animal cloning, there would still be the awesome question of how one would deal with the 'mistakes'.

Psychologically, too, there would be potentially serious difficulties for the child. There would be the 'genealogical bewilderment' of anomalous genetic relations to their parents (one only too closely related, the other totally unrelated?), grandparents (or should one say parents?), and siblings (or are they nephews and nieces?). Of course, in a world where family relationships are increasingly fluid, people find themselves having to negotiate domestic circumstances that are fraught with emotional and genealogical complications, and many do so successfully enough. But it is one thing to make the best of a situation that is less than ideal, another deliberately to create one.

More importantly, there would be the problem of living in

the shadow of one's clone-parent. Not only would a clone-offspring be likely to know rather precisely what they were going to look like over time; they would also constantly have to navigate their identity over against that of their older identical twin. Certainly it has come to be widely recognised that while a clone would be genetically an identical twin, they would have experienced a different environment from their clone-parent, from the womb through to family and wider influences. As a result they would be expected to differ in substantial ways from their clone-parent. Yet growing up is in good part about negotiating an individual identity and learning independence from one's parents. This is a complicated business with the fairest of winds, but would be immeasurably more so if it also required traversing the psychological cross-currents of being expected to conform to certain ideals embodied in an elder twin. It would be bad enough if that twin were a dead sibling, and a child had been created precisely in order to duplicate them. It would be even worse if the clone-parent were also the social parent, with the added emotional power that such a position gives.

All of these points are ones that ought to weigh strongly against the idea of cloning for children. So too are the issues about the commodification of children which we discussed in relation to PGD; these are at least as relevant, and probably more so, in relation to reproductive cloning. But, aside from wider problems with a generalised right to reproductive freedom, which cannot be discussed here,[8] there are also other problems with cloning which concern those who view pro-creation from a Christian perspective. For example, the Christian tradition has always affirmed a connection between having children and the committed, faithful relationship between persons exemplified in marriage. Children are the fleshly embodiment of the one-flesh relationship (Gen. 2:24). The separation of the 'procreative' good of marriage from its 'unitive' good has always been regarded as questionable. For some traditions (notably official Roman Catholic teaching) this requires that 'every marital *act* ought to be open to new life', with a corresponding rejection of contraception; for others (including many Protestant churches) it has implied simply that the *spheres* of sex and procreation should not be put asunder. But whatever view is taken on that issue, it has generated a distinction between using technology to *assist* the role of sex in procreation, which has typically been regarded as acceptable, and using technology to *replace* the role of sex in procreation, which has typically been treated with suspicion. Of course, it is not always clear whether a particular reproductive technology is assisting or replacing sex – there is a spectrum of possibilities between the two. But there is no question where cloning comes on that spectrum: after all, no new sexual act of any description whatever takes place. Indeed, it is difficult to imagine even in principle what kind of reproductive technique could have less to do with sex than cloning. The relational and embodied origins of begetting children, which are expressed in sexual intercourse, are in cloning almost entirely abandoned.[9]

Christians have further reason, therefore, for being grateful that legislatures around the world have begun to move towards the criminalisation of cloning for children. Even if the alarmist scenarios stay firmly in the realm of science fiction, a firm understanding of the realities of human cloning has rightly made clear its moral unacceptability.

Stem-cell research

The same has not been true, however, in the case of 'therapeutic' cloning and stem-cell research. In 2001 the United Kingdom became the only country in the world explicitly to permit research with human embryonic stem cells. The Human Fertilisation and Embryology Act 1990 permitted licensed research on human embryos up to 14 days of development, but did not allow the Human Fertilisation and Embryology Authority (HFEA), which was the regulatory authority created by the Act, to license research on embryos for tackling diseased or damaged tissues or organs. Acting on the recommendations of the Donaldson Committee, the official committee set up to consider the matter, and encouraged by a wide range of patient support groups and medical and scientific associations such as the British Medical Association and the Royal Society, both houses of Parliament finally voted in favour of stem-cell research.

Stem cells are the cells from which all the different kinds of tissue in the body originate. Isolating and cultivating those cells is therefore potentially an important way of developing replacements for diseased tissues or organs: by introducing healthy replacement cells into heart muscle, for example, the damage caused by a heart attack could be repaired. Embryonic stem cells are like ordinary tissue stem cells, except that they are produced at an early stage in embryonic development and have not yet specialised into a particular kind of cell. The aim of the research is to extract them from the embryo, with a view to placing in culture and exposing them to a molecular trigger which might differentiate them into the required cell type. Cloning would be essential to the process inasmuch as it allows the recipient of such cultured tissues also to have been the donor, thereby ensuring a genetic match with no risk of tissue rejection or need of potentially harmful immunosuppressive drugs. In the long term, the hope is that enough will be learned about reprogramming cells so that adult cells could be used without resort to embryonic stem cells.

The proclaimed benefits of the science are certainly significant. In addition to replacement heart muscle, it might be able to produce sheets of skin for burn victims or neurons for those suffering from Parkinson's or Alzheimer's diseases. It might help a patient's pancreas to produce natural insulin, tackling diabetes at its root. By producing 'spare part' organs (in the longer term), it might ease the problems caused by the shortage of donor organs. Mitochondrial diseases, which are often debilitating conditions transmitted through small stretches of DNA found in the mother's egg outside the egg nucleus, could be prevented.[10] It might assist research into the origins of cancer, as well as potentially contributing to the continuous rejuvenation of organs – and thence to the indefinite extension of human lives.

In response to these developments, the first question to ask is whether it is necessary. There is evidence that stem cells can be obtained from a variety of sources other than embryos (or aborted fetuses, which have been the other main source of stem cells to date). Adult stem cells from leg muscles have been used to treat a patient with heart damage following a series of heart attacks. Blood stem cells have been used to restore the blood system in cases of leukaemia, and stem cells taken from umbilical-cord blood after birth are being used to counter sickle-cell anaemia and severe combined immunodeficiency.[11] Many other adult cell-to-cell possibilities are being explored.

Whether embryonic cloning is necessary for stem-cell research is in good part a medical and scientific question. Certainly, those scientists and doctors who have supported embryonic stem-cell research in the British debate are convinced it is necessary. They argue that adult stem cells may have some uses, but that because they are differentiated into tissue types they are in general not as flexible as embryonic stem cells, and therefore not as useful for research or for potential therapies. But the sceptical question whether embryonic cloning is necessary for stem-cell research gains its force at least in part from another quarter. This is the concern that opening the door to embryonic cloning would, over time, inevitably lead to cloning for children. The two may in themselves raise different moral issues, but their connections are such that one will in due course lead to the other.

This could superficially look like a merely rhetorical slippery-slope argument, a fear rooted in moral panic that once the floodgates are opened to embryonic cloning, there is nothing to prevent us sliding all the way down to full pregnancy cloning. Yet labelling something a mere slippery-slope argument is not as such a reason for disbelieving it, any more than asserting that we are on a slippery slope is a reason for believing that we are. Whether an appeal to a slippery slope is justified or not depends on the persuasiveness of the reasons for it.

Here there are a number of factors, of which perhaps the most significant is that the growing safety of procedures that would inevitably arise from increased research into embryonic cloning would reduce one of the biggest single arguments against cloning for reproductive purposes, namely the difficulty that cloning procedures have had in reliably producing live, healthy offspring.

This slippery slope in fact relates to a number of deeper issues about the seeming 'necessity of technology'. This phrase tries to capture a widely held sense that whatever our current revulsion against reproductive cloning and developments in enhancement genetics, it is probably all going to happen anyway. Whether stem-cell research is at the top of (or even some way down) the slope which leads to cloning for children will not be settled forever simply by enshrining in primary legislation the wrongness of full reproductive cloning. It turns on the deeper cultural dynamics which guide our expectations about health, reproduction, and the body, and which finally will overturn laws if they are inconvenient: I address these more fully later, particularly in the final chapter, when we look at the idea of runaway technology. In conclusion, while the potential benefits of stem-cell research are undoubtedly great, the use of embryonic cloning for it could have greater repercussions than might first appear.

The status of the embryo

There is, however, one topic which I have not yet discussed, but which no serious moral account of these issues could avoid. I have not mentioned the question of the status of the embryo so far because it tends to eclipse all other considerations, particularly in the minds of those who think that the embryo should be treated as if a full human person from the moment of fertilisation. This has two unfortunate consequences. To those who do not share that position, it makes those who are persuaded by it seem interested only in abstract arguments and absolute principles, not in the needs of real people. To those who do adopt that position, on the other hand, it drains all other considerations of any importance. Yet neither of these need be the case, and so far I have deliberately presented the arguments in a way which is intended to make clear that they stand or fall in their own right, regardless of one's views about the status of the embryo. Of course, for those who conclude that the pre-implantation embryo does not deserve the protection owed to those who are unambiguously members of the species, it may well be that these additional objections to the technologies have no force. However, for those who reach the opposite conclusion, the arguments I have considered so far are still important, even if there are also further powerful and perhaps conclusive reasons for rejecting these techniques, however attractive their medical benefits may be.

Of the genetic techniques I have discussed, the question of the identity of the early embryo is an issue most clearly in the cases of pre-implantation genetic diagnosis and embryonic cloning for stem-cell research, since both imply the deliberate destruction of embryos. But it is also relevant to discussion of germ-line gene therapy, which I have not discussed in detail. For the research that would be necessary to establish the viability of germ-line therapy would almost certainly require the destruction of at least some embryos, while the germ-line therapy itself in practice would likely lead to the discarding of embryos in which the procedure had not been successful.[12] It might be thought least germane to human reproductive cloning, though we should also note that even here embryos would most likely be destroyed both at different stages in the development of the technology and in its clinical application.

At the outset, we should note two points. First, when personhood begins is a moral question, not a scientific one. Of course, it must be scientifically informed and cannot require things to be true which science shows to be false, but it is not as such a scientific question. It is inadequate, for example, to say that because a unique genotype occurs from fertilisation, therefore fertilisation is when a person begins life; one needs to explain

the significance of a unique genotype, and this is a moral under-
taking. Second, we need to clarify the question we are
concerned with, and the terms which will be used. The central
question at stake is that of ontological identity: when does this
life that is human acquire the status of a full member of the
human community? For the sake of argument, I will simply
stipulate that I am going to use the term 'personhood' and its
cognates to refer to this ontological status, though no term is
entirely adequate. Thus our question is: when does personhood
begin?

The conventional Christian position on the status of the
embryo is fairly represented by official Roman Catholic
teaching, and much of the most coherent thinking on all sides
of the debate has been conducted by Roman Catholics.
According to the Catholic Church, respect for life is owed from
the moment of conception. However, it has never taken a final
position on the question of when personhood starts: the actual
moment of ensoulment, when the individual human being is
endowed with a rational soul, remains officially undefined. But
in view of the gravity of the issues at stake, it teaches that life
must be given the benefit of the doubt from conception
onwards. 'From a moral point of view this is certain: even if a
doubt existed concerning whether the fruit of conception is
already a person, it is objectively a grave sin to dare to risk
murder'.[13] While it may be unclear what status the early embryo
has, 'to be willing to kill what for all one knows is a person is
to be willing to kill a person'.[14]

This position adopts a precautionary principle, that embryos
should be given the benefit of any doubt that lingers over their
status. As such it requires showing that none of the arguments
advanced in favour of a later start are morally decisive. There
are a number of such arguments. One of the most widely discussed was first elaborated by an Australian priest, Norman
Ford.[15] This draws on recent developments in the scientific
understanding of the early embryo, particularly about the
capacity of the embryo in the first few days to twin. Until
about 14 days, the human zygote has the capacity to divide

spontaneously into two genetically identical entities, each of which is capable of growing to full maturity. (There is apparently also some evidence that before 14 days these two may be able to recombine into one.) Ford draws on these observations to contend that personhood does not start until after about 14 days. He uses two kinds of argument, a philosophical claim about the nature of individuality, and a scientific one about the origins of an integrated organism. After lengthy analysis, the philosophical argument concludes that 'an individual that was capable of becoming one or more persons could only be a potential person, not a distinct actual person'.[16] After all, how could an individual become two separate individuals and yet maintain its identity? The scientific argument complements this. Embryology appears to show that before 14 days and the appearance of the 'primitive streak', the embryo is more like a mass of undifferentiated cells, each of which is totipotent and could specialise into any cell in the body. Only after that stage does it become an organised whole with the capacity to develop into a unique human individual. For both these reasons, then, personhood should be associated not with fertilisation, but with the primitive streak and the start of cell specialisation.

Another popular argument, a version of which is compatible with the argument from twinning, appeals to developmental notions of personhood. This argument is based on a variety of overlapping ideas. One is that we should not assume that personhood is an all-or-nothing business; it may be something itself which grows and, perhaps, declines. Another is that embryos are not persons, but merely potential persons; they have the potential to become full human beings, but in their primitive state they should not be regarded as having the full ontological status of personhood. Whatever form they take, arguments of this sort recognise the continuity between the early embryo and the grown adult, but are also keen to emphasise the distance from one stage to the other.

Many other arguments have been made for questioning the personhood of the embryo from the point of fertilisation, though I shall mention only two others. Some have been alarmed by the high rates of natural pregnancy loss. According to some experts, 50 per cent or more of pregnancies are spontaneously lost before implantation. It would seem incredible (and not an obviously loving act of a wise Creator) that this many human beings die before even reaching the wall of the womb, let alone the light of day. Others have pointed to the difficulties in saying that personhood begins at the moment of fertilisation, since fertilisation is not a 'moment': recent evidence suggests rather that it is a process which lasts for upwards of 24 hours from initial penetration of the outer egg wall by the sperm until 'syngamy', the pairing of male and female chromosomes inside the fertilised egg.

However none of these arguments are finally decisive. In relation to the issues raised by twinning, a variety of responses have been made. Some have suggested that the occurrence of twinning is an example of asexual human reproduction: one individual has, without resort to sex, given rise to two individuals. Although at first sight this might seem bizarre, it is not, as such, incompatible with the science: it is a philosophical and moral interpretation of the biological evidence. Perhaps more attractively, others have pointed out that while some embryos do twin, the vast majority do not. Even if one accepted that some persons did only come into being at the moment of twinning, that is not in itself a reason for thinking that others did not come into being at fertilisation. Resolving the issues raised by either of these rejoinders would require a sophisticated analysis of the relevant philosophical issues, well beyond what is possible here. But a crude way of expressing the thought behind this response might be as follows: why is our ignorance – or unclarity – about whether there are one or two persons present in the early embryo a reason for thinking that there is no person present? It cannot be assumed that our ontologies of individuality, which are well fitted for dealing with everyday realities, are competent to provide a clear understanding of the nature of the early embryo.

The arguments defending the idea of the embryo as a potential person have also been questioned. Developmentalist views are seductive because they appear to be the most obvious interpretation of the facts of biological development, doing justice to the facts both that embryos do not have all the capacities of grown human beings and yet that they have the potential to develop them. Yet those facts are equally compatible with the idea that the early embryo is not a potential person, but a person with potential. The idea that it is merely a potential person, and therefore not at that time an actual person, gains its force from an identification of personhood with particular characteristics that we associate with full humanity, such as the capacities to reason, relate to others, exercise choice, feel emotions, and so on. But such capacities are not found to the same degree in all adults: while this may be grounds for recognising that people differ in their capacities (some may be more rational or better at relating than others), it is not grounds for denying or qualifying their status as persons. The same is as true for embryos: that they may not have the capacity to *take* an interest is not a reason for denying that they *have* an interest.[17] Once the connection between personhood and the possession of certain characteristics is severed, the appeal of the developmentalist approach is dramatically lessened. Of course, one can persevere with maintaining the connection, and accept the implication that those whose capacities are dimmed (whether because of their very old age, very young age, mental impairment, or whatever) have diminished rights to be called full persons. But if the history of the twentieth century taught us anything, it is surely that along that path true inhumanity definitely lay.[18]

The argument from spontaneous wastage of unimplanted embryos is finally a matter of theodicy and some of the more speculative parts of Christian doctrine. However, it is important to note that at many periods in history the mortality rates of children in the first year of life have been of similar proportions, and their personhood should not be up for discussion. Likewise, the fact that fertilisation is a process lasting 24 hours or more is not a reason for denying that personhood starts at a more precise moment. It may just mean that we have to look more carefully: one possibility, for example, is that the decisive moment is when the contents of the sperm have been released into the interior of the egg – from this moment on all the genetic material needed for development is present.[19]

The arguments for delaying the onset of personhood to 14 days or later are not as strong as they might immediately appear, therefore. And this is an important conclusion for our overall argument. For it indicates that there is sufficient doubt about the status of the embryo, and therefore that one should decide in its favour. That is, one should not dare to risk killing what for all one knows is a person. And if that is so, then some implications almost certainly follow. Amongst them are the finally unacceptable nature of any research or treatment which requires the destruction of embryos: this potentially includes PGD, germ-line therapy, reproductive cloning, and any variety of stem-cell therapy which requires embryonic cloning.

To a certain extent people's views on the embryo will be influenced by their views on wider matters: for example, the benefits of embryo research and the morning-after pill, on the one hand, and the dangers of an increasingly eugenic, discriminatory and technocratic culture, on the other. A long-term Christian response will require careful dialogue between those of different persuasions both on these matters and on the narrower questions about the personhood of the embryo. Yet such a dialogue cannot be presumed to be an entirely neutral process. After all, on one view of things it is about *killing*, or at least the serious risk of it. Moreover, it is a dialogue in a context where the underlying cultural trends are all in one direction, as we shall see in later chapters, and those trends are as much open to question as the nature of the embryo itself.

None of these objections to the technologies I have just discussed should distract us, however, from the enormous benefits potentially available through developments in genetic science. With some provisos which I discussed earlier, developments in pharmacogenomics, somatic-cell therapies, and other gene-based treatments are certainly capable of being embraced by the Christian church as a witness to human salvation and the God who saves. Yet it is also possible for some forms of genetic intervention to witness to a rather different source of salvation. When our technologies start becoming means of reinforcing discriminatory attitudes towards disabled people and consumerist attitudes towards children, we can glimpse the beginnings of something morally questionable. When a commitment to bodily healing becomes a desire for bodily enhancement, it may be that we are encountering a step towards a salvation other than that found in Jesus Christ. It is to this shadow side of genetic technology that we turn next, in a discussion of eugenics, genetic engineering, and the distinction between therapy and enhancement.

chapter three

Genetic Enhancement and the New Eugenics

This chapter looks at the moral issues behind positive genetic engineering and 'designer babies'. It traces the history of eugenics in the twentieth century, and shows its relation to the 'new eugenics' of pre-natal testing and abortion. The moral and theological issues about the difference between gene therapy and gene enhancement are also discussed.

GENETIC SCIENCE is not only about providing cures. As is evident from the ready association in the tabloid imagination of the new genetics with designer babies and the like, it is also about intervention in our bodies for further, non-therapeutic purposes. The possibility of genetic enhancements, of positive genetic engineering, opens out a future in which people may be able to choose for themselves or their children bodily alterations at a fundamental biological level. Indeed, it suggests that through technological manipulation, the process of biological evolution could be speeded up and directed to achieve goals chosen by human beings rather than randomly driven by arbitrary genetic mutations. Such power inevitably raises questions of whether it will be used well or otherwise.

In thinking about the moral desirability of genetic enhancements, we do not need to resort to myths such as that of Frankenstein to raise the questions. The history of the twentieth century has created enough bad experiences of its own. This is why any responsible account of the ethics of enhancement cannot avoid the question of eugenics. In this chapter I will start by considering the history of the eugenic movement in the earlier part of the twentieth century, with a view to showing how its ideals have re-emerged in the different form of the 'new eugenics' of pre-natal screening and abortion. This has largely been the negative eugenics of eliminating disability through eliminating all people who are disabled before they are born, a process that cannot but raise questions about its discriminatory nature. But there are also good reasons for thinking that connected social forces could lead to positive eugenic engineering. Consequently the need becomes more pressing to establish an account of the difference between gene therapy (which, I suggested in the last chapter, is morally acceptable, at least in its somatic-cell variety) and gene enhancement.

Eugenics in history

It is conventional for us now to associate eugenic ideas and programmes with Nazi Germany, as if English-speaking and other countries were untouched by such a terrible taint. Most of us do not know all the details of the Eugenic Sterilisation Law of 1933 or subsequent eugenic marriage laws or euthanasia programmes. But we are familiar in general terms with the doctrines of Aryan racial supremacy, the inducements to those of biologically sound stock to have children, the sterilisation of several hundreds of thousands and then the euthanasia of tens of thousands of people with hereditary and other disabilities, the merging of racial and eugenic policies, the language of 'lives not worth living', the active and willing participation of (and, indeed, the initiatives taken by scientists and doctors in) murderous experimentation, and the culmination of it all in the Holocaust.

But to attach the history of eugenics to Nazism alone is to forget that it formed a much broader movement of ideas, one that achieved enormous popularity and influence in Britain, the United States, Canada, Scandinavia, as well as in other parts of Europe and elsewhere. Nowhere outside Nazi Germany did eugenic policies extend to the mass extermination of their victims, but similar underlying principles of the selective breeding of superior individuals and the elimination of undesirable ones enjoyed widespread support in these countries from shortly after the turn of the twentieth century until the 1930s and beyond. Spurred on by leading biologists, and widely discussed in both the popular media and in scientific and philosophical circles, a variety of movements emphasised the importance of heredity and urged the need to improve the biological quality of the population. As a result of their influence eugenic laws emerged, some enacting discriminatory immigration policies, others requiring sterilisation of those who were regarded as mentally incompetent or subject to other hereditary disorders. Although most of these have long been abolished, laws of the latter kind remain on some statute books even to this day.

The father of modern eugenics was the English scientist Francis Galton (1822–1911), who propounded his initial views in an article of 1865. Historically, there had been a number of writers who had discussed ideas of improving the human race: in the fourth century BC, for example, Plato had used the analogy of breeding domestic animals in developing his proposals for the production of citizens for his ideal state.[1] But it was Galton who first put forward proposals for racial betterment based on an analysis of human heredity. Like many of his middle-class Victorian peers, he was haunted by the so-called 'condition of England' question, inspired in part by the fear that the future of civilisation was under threat from the uncontrolled population growth of the lower classes. He was a younger cousin of Charles Darwin, and drew on his cousin's account of evolution by natural selection as well as his own statistical work to argue that intellectual and moral characteristics were passed from parents to their biological children. Intelligent or 'feeble-minded', socially conforming or criminally delinquent, an individual's abilities and aptitudes were a product of their inheritance. This conclusion suggested a solution to the problem of civilisational decline: since social degeneracy was related to biological inheritance of undesirable traits, the future welfare of society could be secured through encouraging the 'desirables' to reproduce, and discouraging the 'undesirables' from doing so.[2] Just as for generations animal and plant breeders had selected for particular qualities, so human evolution could itself now be controlled by human intervention.

Galton's followers elaborated his ideas. A distinction between 'positive' and 'negative' eugenics was developed, the former encouraging reproduction by those of superior social worth, the latter aiming to dissuade their inferiors from reproducing. Some eugenicists followed the Lamarckian principle that environmentally acquired characteristics could be inherited, and so argued that an improved social environment would lead to the biological improvement of future generations. Others believed that social improvement could make no difference to heredity, a view significantly strengthened by the rediscovery in 1900 of Mendel's account of the laws of inheritance, which suggested that individual traits were the product of discrete units of inheritance (what would later be known as genes); for them the solutions to problems of biological decline were to be found in policies of segregation and sterilisation. Birth control became a significant arena for dispute. Initially contraceptive methods were opposed because they prevented middle- and upper-class women from fulfilling their duties to family and the future of the race; however, as the futility of this became increasingly evident, eugenicists turned into enthusiastic advocates of birth control for the masses, in the hope that it would lessen the numbers of degenerates breeding.

Proponents of eugenics soon turned their minds to legislative change.[3] In the United States, in addition to a large number of state laws which restricted marriage by the mentally deficient, the first state sterilisation law was passed under eugenic pressure in Indiana in 1907, with 24 other states following by the 1920s. Most permitted the sterilisation not only of habitual criminals, but also of epileptics, the insane, and the feeble-minded in state institutions. In 1927 their constitutionality was to be upheld by the Supreme Court, Justice Oliver Wendell Holmes arguing, 'It is better for all the world if ... society can prevent those who are manifestly unfit from continuing their kind', and infamously declaring, 'Three generations of imbeciles is enough'. California led the way, and by 1929 had sterilised almost twice as many people as the other states of the union combined.[4]

The connections with Germany did not go unnoticed: the Nazis were inspired by the Californian sterilisation law, and indeed 'regularly quoted those American geneticists who expressed support for their sterilization policies';[5] in return, a senior doctor in Virginia raised the alarm in 1934 that 'the Germans are beating us at our own game'.[6] In Scandinavia sterilisation laws were passed that were similar to the Nazi legislation. While they were not marked by the latter's racist and anti-Semitic dimensions, and were not pursued with the same ruthless dedication, they were to endure: by the 1970s Sweden was to have sterilised about 60,000 people, mostly women. Britain was an exception with regard to the general move towards legalised sterilisation, despite the best efforts of its well-established eugenic movement. Fierce opposition was raised by a number of liberals and free-thinkers, and by the Roman Catholic Church, which instinctively resisted the modernist and reductionist tone of eugenics, and certainly opposed anything which required individuals to be sterilised. The Labour Party, which represented a working-class popu-lation that was more organised than in most countries and recognised that it was the principal target of eugenic efforts, also offered some resistance. As a result British eugenicists rested their hopes instead on the voluntary actions of indi-viduals, who would sacrifice their own desire for children for the good of all.

Eugenics was not the preserve of uncouth Know-Nothings ignorant of science. On the contrary, many of the most dis-tinguished biologists of the day were counted amongst its supporters: the respected geneticist Charles B. Davenport, the most influential of many eugenicist biologists in the United States, set up a major research institute, the Eugenics Record Office, at Cold Spring Harbour, New York; in Britain, Ronald A. Fisher, a highly influential pioneer in statistics and population genetics, was a strong advocate of eugenic measures. Indeed, it is often difficult to separate early work on the science of human genetics from the interest in eugenics, most scientists of the time agreeing that human genetics should work to improve the race.[7] Nor were the proponents of eugenics confined to conservatives. A programme of what was later called 'reform eugenics', which aimed to preserve eugenic goals while ridding them of their anti-egalitarian bias, was led in the United States by the future Nobel laureate H. J. Muller, and in Britain by the eminent scientists Lancelot Hogben, J. B. S. Haldane, and Julian Huxley. Amongst non-scientists also, many social radicals were to espouse the cause with as much vigour as their opponents: George Bernard Shaw, H. G. Wells, Sidney and Beatrice Webb, and Harold Laski were leaders of a eugenising strain of thought that formed a significant element in British progressive thinking.

Perhaps most important for Christians recollecting this history, there was significant church support for eugenics. Although the Roman Catholic Church took a decisive stand against it in Pope Pius XI's encyclical of 1930, *Casti Connubii*, Protestants sounded a considerably less certain note. Across the United States modernising Protestant clergy often regarded support for eugenics as part of a properly rational and progressive religious creed. Even their conservative critics were not immune, despite the association of eugenics with Darwinism: one American Baptist publication of 1914 entitled *The Rights of the Unborn Race* talked of the baby's right to a sound body.[8] In Britain W. R. Inge, the 'gloomy' Dean of St Paul's, became a notorious publicist for the cause, arguing that if eugenics were forbidden, civilisation would deteriorate 'as surely as a miscellaneous crowd of dogs which was allowed to rear puppies from promiscuous matings'.[9] But while Inge might have been embarrassing, he was scarcely alone. In 1912 the Convocation of the Church of England had come out in support of a Mental Deficiency Bill, which (although significantly watered down by the time the 1913 Act was finally passed) contained provisions intended to prevent the mentally deficient from procreating. The Archbishops of Canterbury and York and other senior bishops wrote to the papers in the bill's defence, while in 1929 several bishops signed a petition in favour of sterilisation.[10] Indeed, when the Lambeth Conference of 1930 debated the morality of contraception, speakers on both sides appealed to eugenic considerations in support of their views. Things were not otherwise outside the established church: the Baptist Union passed a resolution in favour of sterilisation in 1935, and other prominent free-church clergy defended eugenic proposals. Only with individuals such as G. K. Chesterton and Hilaire Belloc and their followers was there to be found prominent Christian opposition. For them eugenics was inextricably linked with the rise of modern capitalism.

A new eugenics?

It is worth pausing for a moment to ask why this history is so little known. Why is it that countries such as Britain and the United States, which were once so beset by enthusiasm for the eugenic creed, have now forgotten their complicity in it? Certainly there were to emerge plenty of good scientific reasons for abandoning eugenic programmes as they had been practised. The distinction between genotype and phenotype helped to clarify the role that the environment played in determining how genes are expressed, and thus made evident the contribution that social environment might in principle make to individual behaviour. Careful attention to the principles of Mendelian genetics showed that since most genetically inherited disorders are recessive, and are carried by many more than those who suffer from them, sterilisation of sufferers was a largely ineffective way of ridding future generations of unwanted diseases. Increased understanding of the distribution of genes within populations made clear that disease genes were not respecters of persons, and so highlighted the social and racial prejudices that had been given a spurious scientific gloss by the proponents of eugenics.

But forgetfulness of the history of science and medicine may not be solely due to believing that it is simply a history of intellectual errors that have since been corrected. Other psychological mechanisms may also be involved. For example, it may be that this is an example of scapegoating, the process by which groups purify themselves of guilt by projecting it onto an individual or another group. English-speaking countries, for example, may feel wholly absolved of the guilt of complicity in eugenics because they have been able to place it all on Nazi Germany, a conveniently evil and unquestionably eugenising regime. And because they contributed to defeating Nazi Germany, their distance from eugenic practices seems the more emphatic.

Whether this speculation is justified or not, it is now completely *de rigueur* for scientists, doctors and others working in the area of human genetics to utterly reject any eugenic intention, and there is no reason to doubt their sincerity in doing so. Codes of conduct for genetic counsellors and policy statements by their professional organisations often include statements explicitly renouncing eugenic objectives. Indeed, such is the distance between current medical self-perception and historic eugenics that one can imagine that it is possible for present-day medical geneticists to go a long way in their career without any clear idea how their discipline ever had any connection with something so morally questionable as large-scale coercive eugenic programmes.[11]

Nor are medical professionals alone in thinking themselves far removed from eugenics. Across Western societies as a whole there has been an allergy to state-sponsored programmes of social hygiene and biological improvement, in reaction to the Nazi experience. Liberals concerned about the threat to individual liberties, religious groups anxious to defend human dignity, disability rights advocates, and a multitude of other pressure groups, including no doubt the vast majority of scientists and doctors, would pose a formidable army of opponents to any such proposals. Those commentators who claim that liberal democracies are unlikely in the foreseeable future to adopt any overt programme of legally backed coercive eugenics surely have a point. Indeed, as Daniel Kevles has pointed out, if a eugenics programme of the Nazi kind were a realistic political possibility, there would be many more things to worry about than merely eugenics.[12] Our instincts on some matters are rather finely honed: with eugenics, as with slavery, there are some kinds of things which liberal societies just know they are against. Arguing that modern genetics is simply Nazi eugenics is to ignore the great differences between them; indeed, it is even liable to be counter-productive, since it suggests to the champions of the new genetics that their critics are short on arguments and have had to resort to abuse.[13]

Yet the comparison of eugenics with slavery is instructive. Societies with liberal traditions have become relatively good at ensuring that formal freedom of contract governs labour relations and that coerced labour and other forms of slavery are rejected as infringements of individual rights. But equally they have often been relatively less good at ensuring that conditions of labour are not degrading, or that there is a plentiful supply of meaningful and appropriate work, or that there is some parity of power between the partners in labour contracts. The formal and *de jure* repudiation of slavery has existed alongside what has sometimes amounted to its practical and *de facto* instantiation. Similarly, state-sponsored and overtly coercive eugenics may be regarded as wholly unacceptable in modern liberal democracies. But this rejection of it in theory might still exist alongside the achievement of eugenic outcomes in practice. Despite our blind swearing and disavowals, eugenics may not so much have died as have adopted a new mask. It is in exploring this possibility that a number of writers have started talking of the 'new eugenics', or a 'backdoor to eugenics'.[14]

What might this new eugenics look like? It is not taking place in mental institutions or immigration stations. It is not being promoted by Conferences for Race Betterment or fostered by worries about the future of civilisation. It is not targeted at the poor or based on spurious correlations between biological make-up and social worth. Yet it may still have the same upshot – of decreasing the number of 'undesirable' individuals and increasing the number of 'desirable' ones. The location for the new eugenics is rather the pre-natal screening suite, the genetic counsellor's office, the general practitioner's surgery, the abortion clinic. Through the practices of pre-natal screening and termination of pregnancy for defective fetuses, genetic screening and selective implantation of embryos, and the possible future technologies of genetic enhancement and the like, eugenic ends are being achieved by very different means. While it may be that no one deliberately and consciously intends a eugenic goal for the population as a whole, the result may well be the same.

To be sure, there are a number of apparent differences between this and the old eugenics that occupied the first third of the twentieth century. There is no resort to overt state coercion or use of legal powers to impose direct restrictions on who may have children; instead, as far as the state is concerned, reproductive decisions remain (at least ostensibly) the voluntary choice of individuals. There is no explicit concern for global questions about the future of the race or the deterioration in quality of the gene pool; instead the focus is on individuals and couples making decisions about their own children. There is no targeting of 'others' or assumption of a connection between a person's social background and the quality of their genetic inheritance; instead the target is disease genes, whoever may happen to carry them. There is no appeal to the language of self-sacrifice or responsibility for the public good in encouraging women to have – or not to have – children; instead genetic counselling takes place within the parameters of the reproductive autonomy of the individual or couple, without direct reference to the wider social good. There is much less ignorance about the elements of genetics and the applications of genetic knowledge: instead knowledge of the human genome is expanding at an exponential rate, with an increasingly large battery of tests and procedures following in its wake; and there is legalised abortion, which remains the only 'therapy' available in the vast majority of cases where test results are positive.

Nevertheless, many features of the old eugenics remain in place. The concern to relieve suffering, on the one hand, and the desire to cut costs to medical budgets, on the other, are both important features. And, centrally, there is the 'negative' elimination of unwanted children through the abortion of fetuses with defects or suspected defects, and the search for the 'positive' enhancement of embryos or fetuses through the various trial technologies of genetic manipulation.

Social pressures, individual choices

Some might question whether this should be called eugenics at all. They might accept that superficially the outcomes may be similar, but deny that this is eugenics on the ground that, even if undesirable genetic traits are becoming less frequent and desirable ones perhaps more frequent, the element of coercion is missing. After all, no woman is legally required to have an ultrasound scan, amniocentesis or other antenatal tests. Genetic tests at any stage are voluntary. Embryo screening and pre-implantation genetic diagnosis may only be done with the agreement of those whose gametes are involved. And while people may question whether or in what circumstances abortion is morally justified, nobody in Western democracies seriously questions that if abortion is to be allowed, it must be with the consent of the woman whose body is being invaded. The sting of eugenics is in its curtailment of freedom, these critics would say; and since the so-called new eugenics infringes nobody's liberties, either it is not eugenics at all or, if it is to be called eugenics, it is of a completely harmless variety.

But this is doubtful. To assert that these are therefore the free and unconstrained decisions of autonomous individuals is to ignore the lived reality of those decisions and the social and economic context in which they are made. To see this, consider the various pressures that bear on an individual woman or couple wondering whether to proceed with an affected pregnancy. First of all, they have to wrestle with their own preferences, desires and fears. Parents standardly want to have healthy offspring, and may fear the thought that they may become parents of a child who has a more or less serious disability. They may fear for the child, worried what kind of future he or she will have, what special schooling may be necessary, what opportunities in life will be closed as a result of disability, who will look after the child when they are gone. They may fear for themselves or for the children they already have, that they will be stigmatised or face rejection because of their nearness to someone with a disability, that more time, energy and money may have to be devoted to bringing up a child than they had bargained for, that their cherished hopes for a happy and healthy family future may be lost for ever. They – and perhaps especially the pregnant woman – may fear for their relationship: she may find herself with threats of being abandoned by her partner or husband if she continues with the pregnancy; and even if this does not occur at this stage, the birth of a child who is disabled may be a significant contributory factor to future relationship breakdown, separation, or divorce.

No doubt the extent to which people experience these fears and the manner in which they respond to them is in good part a product of their own social and cultural background. For example, some ethnic groups are more accepting of those with genetic disabilities than others; some may provide more support for the mother; some may evaluate mental and physical differences differently from others. According to one study in the United States, European-Americans have low expectations of family support but depend highly on medical technology, with imaginable consequences for their attitudes to abortion of affected children. African-Americans, by contrast, are more supportive of family members with disabilities and also more suspicious of medical technology, whereas Chinese-Americans, at the other extreme, are highly committed to technological intervention and see genetic abnormality as catastrophic.[15]

Other factors may also influence social attitudes. Networks of support may be less strong than in previous eras: in an increasingly atomised and geographically mobile society, members of the wider family, who might in previous generations have taken some of the weight of bringing up a child with a disability, may live too far away to be of much practical assistance, while closer friends and neighbours may have their own priorities and commitments. It may be unclear how much support will be forthcoming from financially stretched statutory social services and health services. Technology itself may be contributing towards an increasing intolerance of parents who continue with affected pregnancies. There is some evidence that, whereas in the past having a disabled child was a matter for sympathy on the part of others, in common acknowledgement that it could happen to anyone, an increasingly common attitude now towards those who continue with affected pregnancies is one of disapproval.[16] Precisely because the tests are available and because abortions can be done safely, so the assumption becomes that there is less excuse for having a disabled child. Indeed, the mere existence of a test for a particular disorder creates a pressure on the pregnant woman to take advantage of it.

Perhaps as important as any factor which will bear on decisions to continue with or terminate an affected pregnancy is the role that is played by genetics professionals and by the health service as a whole. While again the rhetoric is one of neutrality and helping women to decide, the reality is rather different. Despite appearances, their role is hardly a neutral one. The range of tests and procedures which a pregnant woman will undergo, for example, from ultrasound scanning through to amniocentesis and chorionic villus sampling, are all strictly voluntary and cannot be required. But that is not the impression that most women who undergo them will receive, and there is good evidence that they are typically unaware of their choice in the matter. Their relation to the process might best be described not so much as informed consent as acquiescence, in which the medical practitioner trades on an assumed agreement with the pregnant woman about what will be the best outcome.

To some extent the training of doctors tends to encourage the attitude of regarding abortion for impairment as an easier option than coping with a disabled infant. This is reflected in their approaches to counselling. While non-directive counselling may be upheld as an ideal, it is less clear how much it happens in practice, or even to what extent it is possible.[17] Not only will obstetricians often be directive in their advice to pregnant women (more so than genetic counsellors), they may be reluctant to perform tests if a woman refuses to agree to an abortion in advance. Indeed, with the background growth (especially in the US) of wrongful life suits, in which a doctor is sued for failing to use every test that was available, the pressure on doctors to order tests also grows. As a consequence of all this, it is perhaps not surprising that accounts such as the following can be found:

> I was pregnant last year and came under severe pressure from every medical professional I saw about my decision to have no tests. Even when I pointed out that they were talking to a disabled person about possibly eliminating her child if it was disabled, they could not see how offensive it was.[18]

All of these various factors will influence how the choices of individual women and couples are structured and managed. They suggest that, far from conforming to an abstract paradigm of informed choice, the felt reality of the practices surrounding the new genetic technologies is more like a more or less subtle form of coercion. Making decisions involves negotiation of a complex network of competing pressures, which people approach out of the particulars of their own social and cultural formation. And these pressures are not neutral. On the contrary, although there are some countercurrents, their predominant tendency is increasingly in one direction: towards eliminating the undesirables. There may be no formal legal coercion, but the experience of being on the receiving end of the exercise of power can be quite as real.

Indeed, there are some broader economic and cultural features that could prejudice social attitudes and individual decisions yet further. In the 1920s most geneticists thought compulsory sterilisation repellent; and yet by the middle of the Depression years a decade later, their views had reversed. Ways of thinking that would lead to one set of policy conclusions in times of plenty would generate something rather more sinister in times of economic crisis.[19] At such moments the ideas which underlie public attitudes become especially potent, their hidden possibilities frighteningly clear. If in times of economic prosperity a culture increasingly resorts to cost-benefit styles of thinking in relation to healthcare policy; if even when things are well it drifts towards placing the emotional and financial costs of bringing up disabled children on individuals and couples; if it increasingly finds individual identity in genetic inheritance and emphasises biological explanations of social difference, the consequences of economic downturn and its accompanying social dislocation could be devastating for those already experiencing significant social disempowerment.[20]

None of this is intended to suggest that our current practices are comparable to Nazism. As I said earlier, simply to identify modern genetics with Nazi eugenics is to fail to attend to the important differences between them. Even if one regards abortion as the killing of an unborn child, as I do, there is still a clear moral difference between a woman's anguished decision to terminate an affected pregnancy because she does not know how she will cope, and the policy of ruthlessly exterminating people with disability because they are not fit to live. Equally, however, to pretend that there is never any kind of coercion involved in current genetics or obstetrics is simply self-deceiving, for all the reasons we have seen. And in general, while there may be no formal eugenic commitment on the part of any individual or corporate agent, it is quite reasonable to talk of eugenics as an 'emergent property' of the current situation, the achievement of the outcome of improving the population despite the lack of an overt eugenic intention.[21]

Reconceiving disability

If we are seriously to question the emergent eugenics and to lay open the forms of power it engenders, we need to make explicit some of the ideas which underlie it and which influence the attitudes of potential parents, medical professionals, and policy-makers alike. It would be possible to do this by considering the impact of new genetic knowledge on any one of a number of minority groups. Gay and lesbian groups and ethnic minority groups, for example, have been particularly concerned at the way in which the new genetics could be used to reinforce social prejudices they experience. I will, however, concentrate on issues of disability, for two reasons: first, people with disabilities remain the least noticed and least publicly visible of minorities; second, current practices of ante-natal screening and the like are already targeted at disability – no speculation about the future is required.

Public perceptions of disability are shaped by two principal beliefs. The first is that to be disabled is to suffer. Since the relief of suffering is taken in the modern world to be a moral imperative, it follows that the suffering experienced by those who are disabled is something which should be reduced or prevented altogether. The form that this avoidance of suffering takes is strongly influenced by the second belief, that disabled people are a significant cost both emotionally, to those who have to care for them, and financially, to family budgets and the public purse. Reducing genetic disease therefore solves two problems at once: it relieves suffering, and it is less costly in terms of personal commitment and economic outlay.

This is to state the two beliefs crudely, but not inaccurately. Yet this brief statement already contains a number of unwarranted assumptions which disability writers have been keen to contest. For example, it fails to make any distinction between impairment and disability. By contrast with medical models of disability which focus on disability as centrally a medical problem, more recent writers have developed a social model of disability, which makes clear that disabled people are handicapped more by social discrimination and prejudice than by their medically defined impairment. Marginalisation through public invisibility or the imposition of categories of disability devised by the dominant society, unwillingness to allow disabled people their own voice whether in everyday encounter ('Does he take sugar?') or public policy debate, and the myriad of more and less subtle ways in which people with disabilities are excluded from power, from difficulty of access to buildings to discrimination in education and employment; these are often considerably more effective barriers to participation than the physical or intellectual impairments which give rise to them in the first place. This is not to deny that there are levels of impairment, a mistake which advocates of the social model sometimes lean towards, but it is to relocate the source of the problems that people with disabilities face.

It also fails to think about the nature of disability and of disease in general. Disabilities are often names given to cases that tend to the extremes of natural variation, part of the spectrum of abilities and not the categorical difference with the overtones of freakishness which the idea of genetic mutation can give rise to. All human beings suffer impairments of one kind or another: a central moral task is that of recognising the continuities rather than the differences between those of differing abilities.

Disability is not inevitably a tragedy, as both common and professional thinking would tend to imply. There is no simple correlation between level of function or ability to perform and quality of life: while people with conditions such as spina bifida or achondroplasia may experience certain limitations, they would typically describe themselves as healthy rather than sick, and certainly not as hindered (at least by their impairment) as might commonly be imagined. Even the financial arguments are not as persuasive as might be thought: 90 per cent of childhood impairments occur at or after birth, rendering the savings made possible through strenuous programmes of pre-natal testing and abortion relatively minor. Those who are disabled make their own contribution to society neither in spite of their disability, nor because of it, but amongst other reasons because, in conjunction with their disability, they characteristically have resources of personality, talent and humanity which reflect their equal membership of the human race.[22]

Therapy and enhancement

I have approached the question of therapy and enhancement through this discussion of eugenics because ideas of genetic enhancement are being proposed in a specific context. This context is one in which there is a significant eugenic factor. In a weak, non-formally coercive sense, eugenics is a reality in Western societies even now, as many of those on the margins of mainstream society are aware. Precisely because this is the case, even in times of economic abundance, it is not possible to rule out the return of eugenics in a strong, coercive sense – it is perhaps only a Depression away. Thinking about genetic enhancement cannot be done in isolation from this kind of consideration, just as ethics in general, if conducted in abstraction from the power dynamics and felt realities of the world it claims to be addressing, is liable to be self-deceiving and irrelevant.

Acknowledging the forces that have led to the subtle coercion of the new eugenics also enables us to recognise that a similar and overlapping set of pressures may be leading us towards genetic enhancement. To establish this, I want to consider the four human desires that are driving many of the developments in the new reproductive technologies and new genetics: the desire to have *a child*, the desire to have a child *of one's own*, the desire to have a *healthy* child, and the desire to give one's child *the best start in life*. These four desires are, of course, perfectly normal, in the sense that they are both widespread and culturally approved. How strongly any individual feels them, and how they are interpreted and negotiated, will no doubt be influenced by the circumstances of that person's overall formation: individual desires, as we noted earlier, are socially mediated. But they are culturally potent: as a result of them, in the context of powerful new technological developments and an increasingly pliable moral climate, there is coming into being the new world of consumer reproductive genetics.

The first and second of these desires, the desires to have a child, and a child of one's own, are driving the technologies for circumventing infertility: *in vitro* fertilisation, egg donation, gamete intra-fallopian transfer, and so on. As the language of genetics gains an increasing grip on Western cultural imagination, so the desire for a child 'of one's own' becomes interpreted as the desire for a child genetically related to oneself. The third desire, to have a healthy child, is answered by the quite proper therapeutic and preventative medicine associated with early childhood, from open-heart surgery in order to repair a hole in the heart, to immunisations at the local medical practice. But it has also generated the new negative eugenics targeted at disability that we have just explored. And when the desire for a healthy baby surreptitiously slips into the desire for a 'perfect' baby, it is opening up a new vista, not merely of removing 'imperfections' but of positively choosing a particular outcome for one's child.

This vista is given more substance through the fourth desire, to give one's child the best start in life. Parents invest an extraordinary amount in the attempt to give their children the best start they can, from the choice of partner with whom to have children, worries during pregnancy about diet and avoiding smoking and drinking, concerns for the child's physical and mental well-being, expenditure on educational toys, sports equipment or private schooling, to passing on accumulated wisdom about how to make the most of life. Why should those same parents not extend their efforts not merely to the environment in which a child is brought up, but also to the genetic make-up which the child receives in the first place?

After all, if the role of biology in an individual's abilities and behaviour is as important as the language of the genes would have it, then the prospect of genetic enhancements for one's children would surely be correspondingly attractive. Greater intelligence or sporting ability, greater vivacity or gregariousness, to name some traits that have been claimed to be influenced by heredity, all might be appealing targets for those wishing to give their children the best genetic start in life. Moreover, this desire is set in a specific context, that of a rights-based and commercially-driven culture. When the emphasis on rights is no longer just a defence against an over-powerful state but is also the means by which individuals impose their demands on society (here perhaps as the 'right to give one's child the best start in life'), and when there may prove to be significant commercial incentives over time to produce the technologies for such enhancements, it is clear that there are powerful forces working towards human genetic enhancement.

In response to this, it should be said immediately that most of these developments are an extremely long way off, if indeed they will ever be possible. For a start, they would involve technologies considerably more expensive than the already costly PGD. More importantly, most traits that people might want to positively design for, such as intelligence, are massively complex. Not only are they typically multi-factorial, involving the interaction of genes with the environment in a multitude of ways that have yet to be deciphered. They are also likely to be polygenic – one estimate is that some 3000 genes may be connected with intelligence – such that unravelling the role of each gene and the influence of each gene on others is a daunting and questionably feasible exercise. Moreover, because of the multiple roles that genes have and the multiple ways in which they interact, intervention in somebody's genetic make-up always carries the risk of unforeseen genetic consequences. And in some cases, such as intelligence, it is not even clear that we have a sufficient conceptual grip in the first place on what the precise trait is that one might try to engineer.

For these reasons, it is likely that any genetic enhancements

in any foreseeable future would be minor. Given the uncertainties and the expense, the vast majority of humankind
will continue to have their children in the traditional, fun way,
even if any other way were technically open to them. In
addition, there would no doubt for many people be religious,
cultural or even aesthetic scruples about genetic manipulation.
The idea of an inevitable slippery slope towards a world in
which most people routinely improved their children's intelligence or looks or sporting abilities is not one that belongs to
any probable, foreseeable future. Certainly, it should not be
used as an argument for rejecting the many potentially beneficial applications of genetic technology that we discussed in
Chapter Two.

And yet, if it is wrong simply to extrapolate backwards from
a feared future to a blanket condemnation of present practice, it
is also wrong to ignore those features of contemporary Western
societies which might lend themselves to potentially questionable outcomes. The emphasis on the improbability of a
genetically engineered future can be overplayed. As procedures
in reproductive genetics become more effective, safer and
cheaper – and, of course, massive scientific and medical effort
is directed towards this – so the attractions of IVF and embryo
screening will become greater, and the threshold for embarking
on the course of reproductive technology will get lower. The
cultural drift towards separating sex from procreation, decisively accelerated by the advent of effective contraception and
safe, legal abortion, may also gain a new significance. Sex as a
pleasurable recreational activity is already increasingly separated from the rather more serious business of having children.
Producing children may in turn come to be regarded as too
important to be left to chance: intervention in that process, a
mentality already embodied in the technological assistance
given both to those who are not pregnant but would like to be
and those who are pregnant but would like not to be, may
be furthered in decisions not only whether or not to have a
child but also what kind of child that shall be. And so in due
course some may decide that even relatively minor genetic

changes would be worth it, and if necessary will lobby their governments or regulatory authorities to be allowed to proceed.

Of course, this is speculative. But it is not flagrantly so. This becomes especially clear when we see that this process is a continuation, a drawing out of the logic of what is already beginning to happen. In relation to therapeutic treatments, we saw in the previous chapter how familiar non-genetic methods may be complemented by the development of genetic methods: in due course, for example, certain cancers may be targeted not only by the traditional options of chemotherapy, radiotherapy and surgery, but also by gene-based treatments. Similarly, in relation to bodily enhancements we are familiar with a vast number of ways in which we modify our bodies, 'from shaving on', as Karl Rahner put it.[23] We have diets to take fat off or put muscle on, drugs to alter our moods or put hair on our bald patches, surgeon's knives to lift our faces or enhance our breasts. It is easy to see how this might be extended to using genetic means to bodily enhancement.

The possibility of moving from therapy to enhancement is also illustrated by a number of transitional cases which bring out the difficulty in distinguishing the two. Even now, when embryo screening is performed to exclude embryos which are homologous for cystic fibrosis, for example, the question arises concerning which embryos should be implanted. Currently those are chosen which for a variety of reasons are most likely to implant; while this decision is made on grounds which are not connected to enhancement, it is easy to see how over time and with improved techniques for gene analysis this might slip into picking those embryos which are most likely to be healthy. Another example is raised by the possibility of gene-based vaccinations. It might be, for example, that an individual's immune system could be genetically altered so as to protect that person from AIDS or cancer.[24] But it is not clear whether that would count as a genetic therapy, since it is clearly health-related, or as an enhancement, since it would be improving a body's general functioning.

Whatever may be the case in any single example, there are

pressures towards genetic enhancement which cannot be ignored. For many kinds of enhancement, expectation of their advent can be postponed into the indefinite future, as we have seen. Yet the desires to have a child genetically related to oneself, to ensure that it is healthy and to give it a good start in life, when further formed by a consumerist and rights-based culture, push things in a particular direction. In the context of a widespread popular belief in the significance of genetics for personal identity, a mentality that looks for technological solutions to problems, and an economic environment which rewards those who find such technological solutions, the tendency of the culture as a whole becomes clear. Whatever the immediate problems, the theory and potential practice of genetic enhancement is not going to disappear.

Is enhancement wrong?

Why should we worry about the trend towards genetic enhancement? Isn't opposition to it just based on the 'yuk factor', the instinctive revulsion people often feel in relation to new technical developments that impinge on the body? There is no doubt that many people do have such a reaction, whether or not they can give it any rational justification. And yet similar feelings have been expressed in relation to a large number of similar medical advances. Smallpox vaccinations, for example, were greeted with horror in some quarters, as were heart transplants. But in all such cases, after the initial shock, the procedures gradually became increasingly widely accepted amongst the public at large as their benefits became more apparent. The 'yuk' response may not be so much the articulation of timeless moral reason as the product of a variety of other factors, centring on fears about intervening in the body.

Moreover, a critic might add, all these developments can be understood in a rather more positive way. For a start, they increase choice and leave less to fate. As the bioethicist John Harris puts it, in relation to positive enhancements:

It seems to me to come to this. Either such traits as hair colour, eye colour, gender, and the like are important or they are not. If they are not important why not let people choose? And if they are important, can it be right to leave such important matters to chance?[25]

On the assumption that such manipulation is both possible and safe, giving parents more control over such matters is surely a reasonable extension of the parenting role. Harris also questions whether there is any significant moral difference between improving a child's educational environment and altering its biological constitution:

is it somehow evil (or fascist) to wish to improve or even (heaven forbid) attempt to improve the intelligence of our children? And if . . . it is not wrong to attempt to improve something like intelligence by education, why should it be wrong to attempt to improve it by genetic manipulation?[26]

In terms of its moral implications for human intervention, there is no category of 'Nature', if by that is meant something that human beings should not attempt to modify:

If it is not wrong to hope for a bouncing, brown-eyed, curly-haired, and bonny baby, can it be wrong deliberately to ensure that one has just such a baby? If it would not be wrong of God or Nature to grant such a wish, can it be wrong to grant it to oneself?[27]

If alterations in an individual's genome can be made which either are for that person's good or do not contravene any compelling moral principle, then there is no reason for prohibitions against them. And, in general, if the result of genetic manipulations is that people live longer, happier, healthier lives, it is hard to see what might be the objection to them.

The idea that the distinction between therapy and enhancement is unsustainable might be supported by a variety of other considerations. Psycho-socially, the personal consequences of what is conventionally defined as disease may be little different from what is conventionally defined as natural. One person may be very short, for example, because they suffer from a deficiency in human growth hormone, while another has no physiological disorder but simply is at one extreme of the spectrum of natural variation for height. Both may experience very similar social disadvantages, yet it might seem unfair if one was eligible for treatment because they had a specifiable disorder while the other was ineligible because they did not. From an evolutionary point of view too, the claim that a particular level of physical and intellectual attainment is natural and that any advance on it is unnatural and to be avoided is questionable. If evolution is a matter of random mutation and adaptation to environment, it seems arbitrary to privilege one moment in the process of human evolution as the point beyond which no further developments may be made. Philosophically, too, the problems in asserting the distinction reflect a fundamental difficulty in defining disease. This can easily go along with a certain kind of post-modern debunking of categories: the distinction between biological and non-biological improvements to people just reinscribes certain conventional norms which are ultimately arbitrary.

There are powerful reasons, therefore, both for questioning the distinction between therapy and enhancement and for favouring genetic enhancement of at least selected traits. But there are also at least as compelling reasons for opposing genetic engineering. There are basic issues, readily admitted by those in favour of it, about the safety of the procedures and the difficulties of the science involved. We would need to be quite sure that there would be no serious adverse consequences, and that commercial and other interests in bringing a product to market did not mean a blind eye was being turned to potential dangers. We would have to ensure that the tests which would be necessary before a product could be marketed were conducted ethically (and if one believes that embryos should be treated as if human beings, this should include not testing on embryos where that involved their destruction).

Furthermore, some have worried that the process would result in a significant narrowing in human genetic variation as certain genes became especially favoured. They fear that this would have bad consequences for human diversity overall (even though, admittedly, it is not clear that the number of people who are ever going to be in a position to engineer their children will be sufficiently great to make this a serious hazard). Others have with more justification pointed to the potential for great evil that such technological powers might have if they got into the wrong hands.

Clearer and more immediate objections have been raised from the direction of social and cultural studies. Amongst sociologists and social theorists in general there has been a recurrent concern that the massive increase in biological understanding brought about by modern genetics has legitimated a thorough-going effort to explain social behaviour in biological terms. Sociobiology has had the mission of replacing traditionally favoured sociological explanations of behaviour (for example, the Marxist emphasis on economic and class relations) by evolutionary explanations (notably, the neo-Darwinian emphasis on selfish genes). Alongside it, behavioural genetics has looked for the genetic component in behaviour and tended to accent it at the expense of social or psychological explanations: behavioural geneticists tend to emphasise the role of genes in aggressive behaviour, for example, where other human or social scientists might look to family environment or social background for clues. The upshot of this emphasis on the biological dimension is the belief that problems might be better ameliorated through genetic intervention than through social change, a belief that is reinforced by our Western cultural fixation on defining problems in ways such that technological solutions take on a certain air of necessity. And yet if there is a substantial environmental dimension in the vast majority of human behaviours, it would be premature (to say the least) to assume that the only way problematic behaviours can be effectually addressed, or more attractive human traits developed, is through genetic intervention. The search for more valuable human ways of living would be dangerously narrowed if it ever came to over-emphasise genetic manipulations as the means to it.

I am going to return to questions of social justice and the ways in which technology structures our patterns of thought, in the following two chapters. What I wish to develop in the remainder of this chapter are some specifically theological concerns with positive genetic enhancements. While theological considerations have been implicit throughout this chapter, it is now time to make some of them explicit.

Theologically, the central issue which human genetic manipulation raises is about the nature of salvation. To see this, we should consider an ancient theological teaching which the early church fought against, but which has reappeared throughout Christian history in a variety of disguises. Gnosticism, an amorphous set of ideas that shadowed the early development of Christian doctrine, had a variety of strands but a number of overlapping beliefs. The material world, it was commonly held, is evil; it is the creation of a Demiurge, a being who is divine but nonetheless different from the God of redemption. Because matter is evil, neither the created world nor the human body can be good, constituted as they are by physical matter. Jesus Christ, it follows, cannot have come 'in the flesh'; he must have been a purely spiritual being, his humanity merely apparent. Salvation likewise is a question of one's spirit being freed from its ensnarement with matter: it is redemption from the created order to the life of pure spirit. This contrasts with Christian orthodoxy, which maintained the Jewish insistence on the goodness of creation and refusal of any body–soul or spirit–matter dualism, but also argued for the identity of God the Creator with God the Redeemer and for the full humanity of Jesus Christ, and concluded that salvation was in some sense a matter of the redemption *of* creation rather than redemption *from* creation.

What do these relatively abstract theological points have to do with the twenty-first-century problematics of genetic engineering? The issue at dispute between gnosticism and orthodox Christianity with regard to the body was, and remains, something like this: is one's true self to be found in separation from or identification with one's body? Gnosticism gave the former answer. It held the dualist view that the spirit was to be separated from the body. Ethically, this might have the consequence that the body be treated with licentious abandon, since the condition of the body made no difference to one's moral purity (the 'antinomian' alternative); or that it be rigorously controlled in order to demonstrate one's moral worth (the 'legalist' alternative). Either way, the body was separate from one's true self. It was something that could be objectified or treated instrumentally. Within this view the idea becomes intelligible of the body as something which can be made indefinitely malleable to suit the self's ends, which can serve as raw material to be improved. The body is open to being seen as inherently faulty, needing human intervention to perfect it. Within the orthodox Christian view, by contrast, the physical body is something which is inseparable from the self. For Christians the process is more nearly that of learning identification with one's body rather than separation from it. Human bodiliness is something to be inhabited as the creation of a good God. Finitude is not to be regarded as an obstacle to true fulfilment or as something which is to be opposed or feared, nor is it the imposition of limitations which it is the task of human endeavour to transcend.

It does not follow, however, that Christians are committed to a certain kind of passivity because of their acceptance of human physical createdness. On the contrary, they are called to participation in God's action of restoring and redeeming the created world, and one of the central features of this is the practice of medicine, as I argued in Chapter Two. There is, in other words, a proper role for therapeutic intervention against disease and bodily disorder, as a sign of the Kingdom which is the restoration and fulfilment of creation. But if this is so, somehow a distinction needs to be made between those activities which are genuinely therapeutic, and those which, in a more gnostic spirit, amount to efforts to transcend the created order. Despite the difficulties we have already seen, and although the distinction still needs to be properly located, some kind of distinction between therapy and enhancement is at the heart of Christian claims about the nature of human beings and the meaning of salvation.

One way of getting at the question is to ask about suffering. What kinds of suffering may we properly oppose, and what kinds should we properly learn to accept? What kinds of suffering are the appropriate realm of medicine, and what kinds of suffering would it be wrong for medicine to try to banish? The tendency of the modern world is to find this kind of question virtually unintelligible. Our assumption is that all suffering is pointless and to be avoided, and that learning to accept suffering is something to be done only when there is no other option.

But this is a superficial response. As it stands, it can fail to recognise that there are some kinds of pain which are necessary means to our goals: the physical pain barrier an athlete has to cross in training or the discomfort felt by the person trying to lose weight or get their body into shape ('no pain, no gain'). It fails to see those kinds of suffering that may be a consequence of moral commitments we have: the persecution undergone by dissidents against tyrannous regimes or the harassment experienced by whistle-blowers at work acting on conscience. More importantly, even if these are not strictly examples of suffering (since the reason for the pain is evident), there are also different varieties of *pointless* suffering which the modern response fails to distinguish.[28] Not only is there seemingly pointless suffering which medical science can cure. There is also pointless suffering which medical science cannot at this time cure, such as that connected with many mental disorders. And there is pointless suffering which can only be eliminated or 'cured' using morally questionable means, such as eliminating the sufferer through abortion or euthanasia. The modern response runs the danger of absorbing these latter two varieties of pointless suffering into the kind of suffering which can be cured. But not only does this create greater pressure to adopt means such as abortion or euthanasia, giving them a greater air of 'necessity';

it also gives greater credibility to the idea that all suffering is unnecessary.

The idea that suffering is unnecessary prevents us from facing up to the reality of our human condition, which is that suffering for some people for much of the time, and for all people for some of the time, cannot in practice be removed. The more we hide that truth from ourselves, the more terrifying become those times when we are reminded of it. And so in our desperate effort to escape it, we summon up the powers of medicine and medical science, asking them to be our saviour and rescue us from our bodiliness and finitude.

Yet there is a connection between our fear of suffering and our failure of compassion. If avoiding suffering is one's highest aim, one will never be truly open to the suffering of other people. The task of medicine is not to be seduced by the ideal of absorbing all suffering into that which can be cured, but rather to be one form that our love for each other takes when we are suffering. Learning to live with each other and to care for each other in the midst of suffering, overcoming our fear of the suffering of others, refusing the temptation to repress the reality of pain: these are some of the meanings of loving one's neighbour as oneself. It is in this context of the priority of care that such cures as medicine can muster should be placed.[29] It is still open to medicine to refuse the salvific role our culture longs for it to fulfil, and to earn an honest living, truthfully owning up to its limitations and helping people to come to terms with them.

Learning to embrace our limits is an essential part of being human. This is why people with disabilities, rather than being marginal, are essential to a community's moral identity: they embody in an acute and sometimes startling form the limitations which all human beings have. It is also why it matters how disabled people interpret disability, how, as it were, they 'perform' their disability. Quite rightly, much recent writing in the disability movement has rejected the necessary correlation between disability and suffering. As we saw earlier, impairment must not be regarded as inevitably tragic: a person with an impairment may find ways of coping with the problems they face with no greater difficulty than an able-bodied person, may suffer no greater levels of pain because of their impairment, and may enjoy no less fulfilling a life. There is, however, a temptation to push the logic a step further and assert that disability is never suffering and never has a tragic dimension. But this would be a less desirable step to take. One reason for questioning it is that it is simply untrue: there are different levels of disability (even if categorising them should not be done glibly), and some do involve considerable pain and disem-powerment.[30] Perhaps a more important reason is that by denying suffering and putting people with disabilities on a level with able-bodied people, it reinscribes the norms of the dominant society instead of questioning them. It implicitly endorses the right of able-bodied society to define acceptable human life as one which does not involve suffering, and asserts that disabled people ought to be able to live up to those ex-pectations. While the demand for inclusion may be an under-standable and indeed necessary strategy for people with disabilities facing the hostility and indifference of a handicap-ping world, it is arguably also a way of discounting the opposite truth, namely that the expectations of avoiding suffering are unreal for everybody.

Disability, in other words, is a reminder that none of us is all right. Much of our time is spent shoring up fragile identities of normality, which can be shattered in a moment. Against our idealised images of perfect human beings, whether in ourselves or in our children, people with disabilities serve as the raw exposure of what we fear and therefore repress. Indeed, pre-cisely by telling us again of our common condition, our shared vulnerability, the presence of overt disability breaks down the distinction between those of us who identify themselves as disabled and those of us who do not. In this light our shared humanity, whatever our particular abilities and disabilities, takes form in our shared recognition of need.

The question for the project of positive genetic engineering of human beings, then, is whether it becomes the attempt to remove ourselves from suffering, rather than helping us to face up to the truth of our condition. To the extent that it is the former, it represents the effort to deny our common human fragility which is manifested to us by those who are disabled, and with that the abandonment of the Jesus who had no form or comeliness that we might look at him, who was despised and rejected.[31]

Resurrection and the resurrection body

Yet the Christian Gospel is not just a matter of learning that we have limits, that we will die, that we are not God, that we are possessed by fears whose names we try to forget, that we are body–soul unities. All of these are true, but as they stand they are sub-Christian. The Christian Gospel is rooted in proclamation of the resurrection of the one who died. It was the Christian belief in the resurrection of the body rather than the immortality of the soul which acted as the starting-point for the affirmation of creation, including the physical body, and the repudiation of the gnostic complex of ideas. Christianity was launched not by the assertion of an abstract philosophical principle of body–soul unity, but by the experience of resurrection life.[32]

Indeed, it is questionable to what extent we should warmly embrace human limitations without a murmur of protest. There is surely truth in the thought that we should rage against the dying of the light, that death in itself is a kind of affront to human dignity.[33] We should not pretend that pain is anything other than painful – ponder for a moment one father's description of genetic illness: 'to experience genetic disease in one's children is to be immersed in a boiling cauldron of almost pure pain, with a generous helping of surprise, confusion, disappointment, anger, and guilt thrown in.'[34] For many people in the terminal stages of painful illness, escape from the body can only be regarded as an utterly reasonable thing to long for.

Even if, as I have argued, we should be opposed to the attempt to transform medicine from a therapeutic enterprise into the mission of releasing human beings from bodily frailty, it is scarcely an unintelligible thing to want to do. The desire for transcendence of human finitude cannot be construed as an entirely alien aberration.

It is a complex question, and one I will not attempt to answer here, whether it is psychologically and spiritually possible to accept our limitations without some thought of transcendence of them.[35] At all events, for Christians it is the resurrection which sets the context for addressing the question. Beyond any of our hopes, dreams, projects, or anything we might aspire to achieve, all of which end with our death, the resurrection tells us of a new life which will be given to us in which our true humanity will be realised. Human life will find its living fulfilment, even its true limitlessness, in relation to God. Transcendence is set in a new key: not as escape from embodiment, but as the hope of a transformed body. In this hope of a time when sorrow and sighing shall flee away is to be found the power to enable us to rejoice despite the weakness of our bodies. This also creates room for the positive appropriation of suffering.[36] Instead of seeking to deny tragedy, Christians can recognise in suffering the opportunity for discovering God's grace, as we saw in the previous chapter. They can learn to carry each other's burdens, to recognise their need for each other. At times, perhaps often, they will fail to see anything positive in their own suffering or that of others; that, too, is part of the tragedy which they need not seek to deny.

But the resurrection has another significance in relation to genetic manipulation. For the Bible does talk about the radical modification of bodies. The language it adopts is that of the resurrection body, the transformation of all our bodies. What is the significance of this? It would be ludicrously inappropriate to enquire what precise form the resurrection body might take: Paul dismisses those who speculate about this in the single word: 'Fool!' (1 Cor. 15:36). But it is clear that it will be categorically different from the bodies we know, whilst yet somehow being the same body – just as Jesus' resurrection body is one that is able to go through walls, and yet also one that is recognisably him. At any event, whatever the resurrection body is, it cannot be the end product of human manipulation: flesh and blood, however much human beings may intervene in them, cannot inherit the Kingdom of God (1 Cor. 15:50). Rather, the New Testament emphasis is on the transformation of our bodies into bodies that will be fit for the life of the new heaven and the new earth, and that this transformation will be the work of God.

Therapy and enhancement again

This idea of the resurrection body suggests a way of rethinking the distinction between therapy and enhancement. So far I have given some general background reasons for caution about genetic enhancements, and some reasons for thinking that a distinction between them and gene therapies needs to be made. But, while I have mentioned a number of considerations why many have found the distinction questionable, I have not specifically addressed positive reasons for making it.

One of the most prominent recent attempts to specify the limits of just health-care policy has been that of the philosopher Norman Daniels.[37] His 'normal function' account of health defines ill health in terms of deviations below the mean of what a person in their particular reference class (taking into account age, gender, etc.) might expect. He proposes that, in the case of deviations below the mean, interventions which aim to return a person to the mean may properly be addressed through health-care policy, while interventions designed to lift people above the mean are to be counted as enhancements. One practical advantage of this approach is its superiority to 'positive' health models which place health at a level higher than typical functioning, and so enter the quagmire of having to decide the criteria by which health improvements are to be judged. But it faces problems in relation to the therapy/enhancement distinction. Aside from the question of making what is statistically average the criterion of what is normatively healthy, it cannot make sense by itself of the value of preventative enhancements. As Eric Juengst has well argued, health-care-related enhancements such as the genetic immunisations mentioned above will raise a person above the species-typical level of functioning. However, on Daniels's account these would count as unacceptable enhancements, whereas there is at least a strong prima facie case for regarding them as an acceptable part of health care. The normal-function model, in other words, can assert the distinction between therapy and enhancement but provides no criterion for telling when one has crossed the line.[38]

Juengst's own alternative is to argue for the real ontology of diseases. He proposes that, instead of seeing only individual bodies as real and regarding disease simply as a metaphorical way of talking about their abnormal functioning, we should also recognise the reality of diseases in themselves as identifiable patterns of pathology related to particular causes. This would then give a criterion for distinguishing therapy, which addresses identifiable types of malfunctioning, from enhancements, which do not, and it would allow preventative genetic manipulations to be regarded as morally acceptable on the grounds that they assist the body in combating particular diseases. The virtue of his approach is that it captures some of our central instincts about the difference between therapy and enhancement: there is something intuitively appealing in the general idea that medicine should relate to disease and not pander to people's desires for designer improvements. But as Juengst himself recognises, his account still faces problems. It remains difficult to know what will count as disease in many controversial cases. And, since it only deals with what is proper for *medicine* to address, it doesn't answer the question, 'Is anything wrong with genetic self-improvement pursued *without* the help of a doctor?'[39]

In the face of this, it is tempting to abandon the distinction altogether. James C. Peterson argues that instead of using criteria of curing and enhancing, we should draw up criteria for deciding if an intervention is appropriate, and any genetic manipulation would be allowed if it can meet them.[40] He proposes five criteria: that human genetic intervention be incremental, choice-expanding, patient-directed (or parent-directed in the case of children), within societal boundaries, and carried out by acceptable means. These would allow safe and effective gene therapies, but would provide some kind of brake on more expansive genetic utopias. This approach is at least honest about the problems with the distinction, and tries to limit the damage in practice. But it faces problems of its own. Aside from questions about whether it adequately addresses the legitimation that such an approach might offer to potentially rather less benign forms of genetic intervention, it fails to address the ways in which we enhance bodies in line with dominant cultural norms and so reinscribe certain patterns of power through them. Perhaps most importantly for a Christian approach to the issues, it fails to recognise the profound theological reasons for wishing to maintain the distinction.

The key to a theological understanding of the treatment/enhancement distinction lies in the implications of seeing the resurrection body as the decisive, divine transformation of our bodies. The problem with abandoning the distinction is that it ignores the difference between identifying with one's body and separating oneself from it, grounded theologically in the difference between the resurrection of the body and the immortality of the soul. But how might we move from this abstract theological dispute about the body to something that would have some purchase on the concrete questions of genetic intervention? After all, the nature of the resurrection body gives us little clue, as we have seen.

The answer, I suggest, lies in understanding that there is a symbolic dimension to human action. Human actions convey meanings and broader resonances beyond an immediate description of the bare action. In this case, different interventions in the body can symbolise different things, and it could be these broader significations which are morally decisive. Thus it may be that the first question to be asked is not, 'Does this intervention count as treatment or enhancement?', but rather, 'Does this symbolise a recognition of human limits or an attempt to transcend them? Does this admit the transience of our efforts, or does it aim for permanence? Does this show forth our common human need, or is it a kind of false salvation? Is this an effort to show what God is like, or an effort to be like God?' These questions are not so much about individual motivations, though they may be, as about the cultural commitments that are symbolised in particular actions. The danger of the search for a clear dividing line between therapy and enhancement is the reductive assumption that it ought to be possible to read off whether an intervention is therapeutic or not simply by knowing the description of what kind of intervention it is. Rather, the most important contrast is not between species of intervention but between species of motivation and cultural commitment.

One implication of this is an acknowledgement that many procedures which are conventionally regarded as uncontroversially therapeutic may well be embarked on in some cases out of a desire to transcend bodiliness. Similarly, it might well be the case in principle that some enhancements could be done in a spirit of the recognition of human limits. While theological emphasis on the resurrection of the body demands some kind of treatment/enhancement distinction, this cannot be immediately mapped onto particular procedures. Rather, it demands that a society reaches a certain kind of self-knowledge, an awareness of the allegiances which underlie its practices. We will consider what this might involve in Chapter Five, when we think about the role of the church in the discernment of cultural trends.

Such a profound task of cultural self-understanding does not lend itself to quick answers about which particular techniques might be acceptable and which not. But by relocating the question of therapy and enhancement, it frees us from being too prescriptive when we come to think about individual procedures. For example, it means that we need not fear a certain amount of apparent arbitrariness. In many other areas of life arbitrariness is unavoidable: the age of consent, for example, or the ages at which people may vote or legally buy alcohol, are cases where a society agrees that a line has to be drawn, whilst acknowledging that to a certain extent it will be arbitrary and might legitimately be regarded as too early or too late for any given individual. To accept an element of arbitrariness in decisions about what will be regarded as an acceptable genetic intervention is not the same as asserting that it is entirely random.

It also allows the kinds of considerations mentioned earlier to take their place as provisional indicators of where a line should be drawn, which would need to be explored in further detail. For example, one guideline might be suggested by attending to the nature of disease, marking off as unacceptable those interventions which could not be related to identifiable physiological disorders. This would allow genetic vaccines, which are genetic interventions, but clearly health related. It might also draw a distinction allowing correction for short height if this were due to genetic disease, but not if it were merely due to being at the lower end of the normal variation for height.[41] Another guideline would concern whether motivations were basically narcissistic or driven by fantasy: this might throw into question some genetic enhancements undertaken for cosmetic reasons. Perhaps the single most important criterion is whether a particular intervention is compatible with a commitment to justice and human community: would it enhance the power and wealth of the few, or would it be available to and beneficial for all? This raises questions we will turn to in the next chapter.

chapter four

Justice, Community and Genetics

This chapter considers how different understandings of justice and the relationship between individual and community bear on some central issues of genetics. In particular it looks at:
- behavioural genetics;
- the use of genetic information by insurers;
- gene patenting.

It also looks at some broader problems of global justice and genetics.

IMAGINE A SOCIETY which was governed by the following set of ideals. People see themselves as individuals before anything else, and cherish their individual freedom above perhaps any other good. They relate to others in many ways – as friends, lovers, business partners, employees, clients, teachers, tenants, and many others – but always in ways that emphasise the priority of individual choice. Consequently they place a great emphasis on individual rights to protect those choices, and on the freedom not to be required to do anything to which they have not consented. They believe in equality, particularly equality before the law, but also equality of opportunity, so that people's talents and hard work are rewarded by financial and other benefits. They also believe that those who are so inclined should give generously to address the needs of others, particularly those who are poor. Nevertheless, equality, and certainly not any kind of equality of economic distribution, would not be as central an ideal for people of this society as liberty and individual autonomy.

Contrast this with a society animated by a second, different set of governing assumptions. People in this society regard themselves as being in a deep sense social beings, formed in a multiplicity of ways by their language and culture. While they may prize individuality and the exercise of choice, this is set within a context of an awareness of the ultimate equality of all, and hence the responsibility of each to each other and to the society as a whole. Those who exercise their talents for economic gain do so in the understanding that their prosperity is also to the benefit of all, and not just themselves. When new scientific or technological advances are made, or when research proposals are being funded, the initial question will be more about how they enhance solidarity and the dignity of all, particularly those who are marginalised from the mainstream of society, rather than whether they will augment or hinder the freedom of individuals. Individual liberty, including both civil liberties and a cultural ethos which promotes responsible choice, is encouraged in this society, but it is placed within a fundamental commitment to the common good.

Societies of these two kinds do not exist in the real world, at least not in the pure, idealised forms which I have just described. Unquestionably, they are crudely characterised. Nevertheless, thinking about these can help us to understand some of the fundamental tensions which exist in Western societies. Both sets of ideals are to be found in contemporary liberal democracies. They are represented by political parties, and may be debated by different strands within parties as much as they are debated between different parties. They are fought over by political philosophers, some arguing that they should be interpreted in ways that are fundamentally incompatible with each other, others suggesting that both can be incorporated into a single schema, and still others attempting to replace them with completely different political conceptualities.

In relation to genetics, they can help us to identify some of the underlying commitments with which Western societies are likely to engage issues raised by the new developments. In this chapter I want to illustrate these contrasting approaches by taking three topics which superficially do not appear to have much to do with each other: behavioural genetics, the use of gene testing for insurance purposes, and gene patenting. In each of these cases, I will argue, there are tensions between a view of society whose hallmark is individual autonomy, and one whose emphasis is on a communal commitment to the good of all. Each of them is presented in a way which allows them to be read as free-standing topics, for those readers who are interested only in one or two of them. But together they form steps in a cumulative argument towards the idea that the appropriate moral motifs for a society wishing to engage seriously with questions raised by the new genetics should be more nearly ones of justice and the common good, than of the autonomy of individuals. In conclusion I will show why the church also has a stake in this view of society.

Behavioural genetics

The first area I want to look at is behavioural genetics. Much of the alarm which has been caused by research in this field has arisen because of fears that we will be shown to be less free than we thought we were, and that our capacity for responsible action will be shown to be irretrievably compromised. A good deal of this is based on misunderstanding, as we shall see, though I will also argue that many of those who have rightly criticised genetic fatalism are prone to an equal and opposite error of their own. But my underlying point, as will emerge at the end of this section, is that concern for a loss of liberty reflects a set of anxieties created by a view of human beings that is more typical of the first of our two societies. The more important moral questions at stake, I shall claim, are about the nature of community and the demands of justice.

Behavioural genetics explores one of the most complex of all questions, the explanation of human behaviour. It is concerned with the role that genetics plays in behaviour, and in particular with understanding the contribution that genetic inheritance makes to behavioural differences between individuals. By contrast with evolutionary psychology, which is another field that attempts to bridge the biological and behavioural sciences, behavioural genetics concentrates not on differences between species considered over long evolutionary periods, but on differences between individuals within a species in current populations. Whereas evolutionary psychology might investigate, for example, how human beings as a whole have developed high levels of intelligence when compared with other similar species, behavioural genetics would study the varying contributions of environment and genetic inheritance to the levels of intelligence of particular individuals or groups.

In order to explore the respective influences of nature and nurture on human behaviour, researchers have not, of course, been able to breed special experimental strains of human beings over several generations, as they have done when studying animal behaviour. Instead they have had to locate those cases in which the experimental ideal of a complete separation between heredity and environment can best be approximated. Two have been most prominent. First, adoption of children shortly after birth allows study of the differences between genetic parents and their offspring who have been adopted by others, as well as of the differences between adoptive parents and the genetically unrelated children whom they have adopted. Adoption studies can also be designed to look at the effects that different family environments have on genetically related siblings who are adopted by different families, or that the same family environment has on genetically unrelated children adopted into the same family, and so on. The second approach has been through the study of identical and non-identical twins. Identical twins (also known as monozygotic twins) are formed from the splitting of a zygote at the very early embryonic stage, and hence share every gene in common. Non-identical twins (also known as fraternal or dizygotic twins) result from the separate fertilisation of two eggs, and so will be on average 50 per cent genetically related, like any two full siblings. Twin studies are typically designed to compare identical and non-identical twins, on the grounds that if heredity is important for a particular behavioural trait, this will become apparent through greater correlations in the behaviour of identical twins.

While both adoption and twin methods had been employed since the 1920s and earlier, they had relatively little influence on psychology as a whole until the 1960s and 1970s, when a series of studies of schizophrenia and other disorders demonstrated some striking results. In the case of autism, for example, it had been assumed for many decades that maternal attention towards the child was to blame (either too much of it, or not enough, depending on who you consulted). In 1977, however, research using the twin method was published which suggested a genetic connection. This was premissed on the assumption that if parental behaviour was responsible, then there should be no difference in outcomes for identical and non-identical twins. If, on the other hand, there was a genetic link, then identical twins should be more likely to share autism than non-identical twins. In the research, ten autistic children were found who were also non-identical twins; the twins of none of these turned out to be autistic, in line with earlier evidence which suggested that overall only about three per cent of autistic children have autistic siblings. However, fifteen autistic children were also found who had identical twins; eight of these were four pairs of siblings, in which both twins were autistic. While the sample sizes were admittedly small, this still represented an astonishing 500-fold increase in risk over the population as a whole, and considerable evidence for some genetic role in autism.[1]

It is one thing to have evidence for some genetic component for a behaviour; it is, however, another thing to be able to assess how substantial that component is. In order to calculate the amount of contribution heredity makes to a trait, behavioural geneticists have developed the notion of 'heritability'. This tries to capture the size of the genetic effect, such that high heritability means that genes account for a large proportion of the variance found in a population, while low heritability means that environment is relatively more important. For example, body weight appears to have a significant genetic component, with a heritability, according to one study, of about 70 per cent.[2] This means that 70 per cent of the difference in weight for the particular population under study was due to the genetic differences between members of that population, rather than to environmental differences such as eating habits or exercise. What it does not mean is that 70 per cent of the weight of every individual in that population is due to their genes and 30 per cent to their dietary habits and exercise regime. Heritability is a feature of populations, not of individuals, and knowing the heritability of a trait does not as such tell us about the respective contributions of nature and nurture in a particular individual. Moreover, heritability is a feature of populations in particular environments: that is, in a different environment heritability of body weight could be quite different, either higher or lower. The significance of these points will become clear later.

All of these features – adoption studies, twin studies, and calculations of heritabilities – form central features of quantitative genetic research into behaviour: that is, the statistical study of the relative influence of heredity and environment within particular populations. This overall approach, elaborated with many permutations in research design and using sophisticated methods of statistical analysis, has for many decades been central to behavioural genetics. In recent times, with developments in technologies of gene sequencing and mapping, it has increasingly been accompanied by molecular approaches which attempt to identify the location on the genome of the individual genes involved in different kinds of behaviour. Thus when researchers claimed in 1993 to have found a marker on the X chromosome which linked with male homosexual orientation, the so-called 'gay gene', this was the product of precisely such a method.

In general, molecular methods adopt one of two approaches. Either they try to correlate particular traits with particular genetic markers through linkage studies: the researcher starts with a trait and then looks for the gene. Or they look at the behavioural consequences when genes are missing from a chromosome: the researcher starts with a (missing) gene and then looks for the trait. In fruit-flies and mice this has been regularly done through 'knock-out methods' – direct engineering of the genome to view the phenotypic results. Whatever the morality may be of such research in animals, there would be obvious moral problems with adopting such methods in human beings. Nevertheless, it is possible to investigate the behavioural consequences when a gene is malfunctioning; and it is this latter approach which is becoming increasingly favoured as a more effective, not to say cheaper, way of learning about gene function.

Links to specific locations on the genome have been claimed for a large number of behaviours: amongst them, bipolar affective disorder (manic-depressive illness), familial Alzheimer's disease, schizophrenia, alcoholism, 'novelty seeking', autism, and attention deficit hyperactivity disorder (ADHD), as well as male homosexuality. But despite the initial excitement, many of these results have also been rejected, or at least heavily qualified, by subsequent research. This has led to the first flush of enthusiasm being replaced in more recent times by a rather greater caution, indeed scepticism, in the interpretation of results. Consequently, very few associations have been relatively widely accepted: a link between late-onset Alzheimer's disease and a particular allele at the apolipoprotein E locus on chromosome 19 is perhaps the most prominent – yet even the detailed interpretation of this is unclear. The science of relating individual genes to particular kinds of behaviour is very much in its infancy, and faces the daunting complexity of disentangling the interactions and correlations between genes and environments for different behaviours, as well as the effects of genes on each other.

Nevertheless, despite the unconcluded nature of the research, the development of molecular approaches has been largely responsible for the rise of the 'gene for' phenomenon in recent

years. Against the broader background of quantitative genetics,
this has led to many of the current fears about behavioural
genetics. Many of these circle round worries over genetic
fatalism and the loss of freedom. For example, if I have the
purported 'gene for' late-onset Alzheimer's, or alcoholism, or
schizophrenia, does that mean that I am fated to get it? If I
have the gene (or genes) which allegedly makes it difficult to
stop smoking, is there any point in my trying to give up? If I
am genetically predisposed towards violence, might this excuse
my delinquent behaviour? If I have a genetically poor intellectual endowment (on the questionable assumption that this can
be determined), is there any point in applying myself to my
education, since I will never be able to obtain any level of
intellectual attainment beyond that which I am pre-pro-
grammed to reach? Indeed, is there any point in working hard
anyway, since if my intellectual abilities are genetically fore-
ordained, then nothing I can do is going to make them any
better, and doing nothing is not going to make them any worse?
The spectre of genetic determinism haunts every newspaper
headline which claims that a new 'gene for' some trait or
another has been found.

But there are also fears about whether knowledge of genetic
predispositions will lead to an increase in prejudice against
particular groups of people. Will isolation of the alleged 'gay
gene' lead to increased abortions and embryo selections in cases
when the offending allele is discovered? Although some
researchers have sought a gene for homosexuality precisely in
order to show that it is 'natural', and therefore not a reason for
discrimination, others fear that in a homophobic society this
would become another channel for the expression of anti-gay
prejudice. Another *cause célèbre*, which was given renewed
notoriety in the 1990s through the publication of Richard J.
Herrnstein's and Charles Murray's *The Bell Curve*, concerns the
question whether there is any connection between intelligence
and social class, and in particular whether there are any
inherited racial differences in IQ.[3] There is evidence for some
difference in average IQ between blacks and whites in the

United States. The question is whether this is due to environmental factors (such as socio-economic and educational
background), or whether it might also imply that blacks are
genetically less well endowed with intelligence than whites;
and if the latter, whether it would justify social policies that
would (amongst other things) give them a smaller share of
governmental education funding on the grounds that they are
less capable of academic achievement.

The stakes involved in questions of behavioural genetics are
clearly very high. In order to understand the issues properly,
we need to return to and develop some of the basic points
about behavioural genetics which I outlined earlier. Perhaps
the first thing to note concerns the status of the scientific
research and the difficulty of achieving results which are likely
to be widely accepted. Newspaper articles, even those in the
'quality' press written by reputable science journalists, will
regularly report the results of single research studies as if they
were the definitive scientific conclusions on the relation
between some gene or genetic influence and some trait. And
yet the disputed nature of the results is one of the most striking
features of research in behavioural genetics.

In the case of quantitative genetics, it is important to
remember that twin studies, adoption studies and other family
studies are difficult to replicate. They are inevitably likely to be
open to some doubt, simply because of sample sizes that are
frequently small and variables that are poorly understood.
Given the different circumstances in which such studies must
take place, it is not surprising that different surveys have produced often wildly divergent estimates of heritability of traits.
Moreover, calculations of heritability depend on accurate separation of genetic and environmental components. But such
calculations are not a straightforward matter of adding together
two discrete items. One requirement, for example, is to separate
out shared from non-shared environments: to distinguish, that
is, those environmental features which serve to make siblings
similar from those which serve to differentiate them (all siblings in a family may have experienced the parental divorce,

for example, but not all may have had the same childhood diseases). Moreover, genes relate to the environment in different ways. Not only in some cases do genes interact with the environment to produce strikingly different phenotypes depending on the environment. More complicated, and more common in behavioural genetics, is the feature that particular genotypes are characteristically associated with particular environments. For example, people with higher levels of intelligence will generally seek out environments where there are other people of similar intelligence; and to the extent that genotype contributes to intelligence, to that extent genotype will be associated with environment.

Needless to say, behavioural geneticists are becoming increasingly adept at taking such complications into account. Yet the levels of disagreement, the disputes over results, and the frequency of contrary findings, all suggest the wisdom of treating the 'evidence' of individual reports with considerable caution.

The same is true of molecular studies in behavioural genetics. Not only are there the difficulties posed by pleiotropy (i.e. that individual genes can have several phenotypic effects) and contingency (i.e. that individual genes may depend on other genes to achieve a particular phenotypic expression). There is also the problem that the method of linkage to genetic markers on chromosomes can only provide a statistical correlation between a genetic location and a behavioural trait – it only indicates the marker (i.e. the general chromosomal position), not the gene itself. Consequently, such associations can be spurious, or at best unproven, even in cases where the phenotype is relatively identifiable (e.g. Alzheimer's disease).[4] When one comes to the more indeterminate traits that behavioural genetics is also concerned with (such as 'novelty-seeking' or other equally ambiguous phenotypes), let alone such complex phenomena as intelligence, the dangers of reaching premature conclusions are even greater. The reason why newspaper reports of genetic discoveries should be treated with a pinch of salt is not just because of their tendency to sensationalise, but also because the scientific research on which they are based may itself be not quite so secure.

The statistical nature of the correlations in both the molecular and the non-molecular approaches also indicates another important feature of such research. Neither knowing heritability nor knowing a genetic marker is enough to give us the whole causal story. Heritability, as we saw earlier, is a population-relative notion, and says nothing about the genetic contribution to a trait in any particular individual. The heritability of breast cancer, for example, is extremely low overall (about ten per cent), but for those who have mutations in the BRCA1 or BRCA2 genes, the odds of getting breast cancer are much higher. Knowing the heritability of a trait does not as such help towards knowing the strength of genetic influence in any individual, let alone towards providing any predictive genetic testing. Even when a locus has been found, the association of it with a trait may be of little or no practical help in predicting outcomes for individuals: the strongest of associations found to date, between ApoE and late-onset Alzheimer's, is still far too imprecise to specify future risk.[5] And a full understanding of the consequences of a gene's interaction with an indefinite range of environments would be required before one could sensibly think of direct genetic interventions.

In the first place, therefore, any assertion of genetic fatalism runs up against the size of our scientific ignorance. But even if our levels of knowledge were much greater, as no doubt they will be over time, there are still other reasons for questioning genetically based fatalism. For a start, to say that a trait is 'genetic' is not to say that it is 'fixed', and to say that it is genetically determined is not to say that nothing can be done about it. Phenylketonuria (PKU), for example, is a genetic condition which results from a single gene malfunction and leads to moderate to severe mental impairment. Yet its effects can be almost entirely escaped through dietary changes which remove sources of the amino acid phenylalanine. That it is a genetic disease does not mean that it is unavoidable.[6] Conversely, that something has been environmentally caused does not mean that it is easily reversible: consider the long-term psychological effects of child abuse. In thinking about determinism, the issue therefore is not whether something is genetic, but whether it is malleable: that is, the extent to which it can be changed. A similar point arises in relation to heritability: in principle a trait that was highly heritable (say, a certain kind of hearing problem) could be very easily compensated for (for example, by a hearing aid). High heritability and a strong genetic contribution are not the same as unavoidability.[7]

The environmental dimension of heritability also brings out another important element of behavioural genetics. Because heritability is defined for a population in a particular environment or range of environments, heritability for a trait may in principle be different if the environment changes. We can illustrate this point through a consideration of the heritability of intelligence. With a number of simplifying assumptions, it is possible to calculate the heritability of intelligence for a given population over a certain size with a particular environment. Imagine now that the environment changes through the discovery of a highly effective 'Mr Memory' educational method, which massively improves the IQ for some people in the population. The genetic contribution to intelligence would remain the same, but the total variance in IQ levels would be greater, and the environmental contribution to overall IQ would be greater. Correspondingly, as a result of the environmental change, the average IQ of this population would be higher, and its heritability of intelligence would be lower. In other words, even if the heritability of intelligence were high in a particular environment, different environments would lead in fact to different IQ outcomes.

This has very important implications for thinking about the relationship between IQ levels and social stratification. Even if intelligence is highly heritable for a particular population in a particular environment, a point which for reasons we explored earlier should not be conceded too readily, this does not mean that actual IQ levels could not be very different for the same population in a different environment, let alone for a different population in a different environment. In principle, therefore, it could be that all variation in IQ between blacks and whites in the US is due to environmental differences, and none at all to differing genetic endowments. And indeed there is evidence that changing environments can very significantly affect IQ scores.[8] In terms of social policy, therefore, there are in principle grounds for investigating educational, economic, and other social factors at least as much as genetic factors in relation to IQ levels – and this remains the case even if the heritability of intelligence turns out to be high.

As it happens, there are a number of other problems in relation to determining the influence of genes on intelligence. One is that there are so many genes involved in intelligence that there is not likely to be a reliable test for the contribution to intelligence of any particular gene. For the foreseeable future the most accurate predictor of an individual's intelligence will remain quite simply the average of the IQ of their parents. More fundamentally, there is still some dispute whether notions such as g, the purported measure of general cognitive ability, pick out a basic, unitary property of the mind; or whether they are simply an extrapolation from measurements of a variety of separable mental functions. While many hold that for all practical purposes there is such a thing as general intelligence, critics still maintain that no single number or IQ score could meaningfully capture the complex range of different abilities lumped together under a simple notion of intelligence.

There are, then, powerful reasons for not being misled into any kind of genetic fatalism, reasons which turn in good part on a proper understanding of behavioural genetics. They are, moreover, reasons for questioning any necessary connection between supposed genetic inheritance and performance in IQ tests.

Yet this is not the whole story of the genetics of behaviour as it is being played out in modern Western societies. It is not sufficient to explain that there are good reasons not to be worried by a reductive genetic fatalism. For a start, it is not the predispositions to particular behaviours in themselves that matter in practice so much as the cultural and psychological impact of people's perceptions that they may be predisposed. People may be able to improve their mental competences enormously, for example, but if they perceive that their inherited capacities limit the amount they will progress, they may be less inclined to try. The real limitations may be as much psychological as genetic.

But behind this, there is something else which needs to be explained. Why is it that our culture is so obsessed with what might be called the myth of genetic fatalism? Of course, particular applications of it can serve particular political needs. It is surely no accident that stories of biological determinism have come to the fore at times when ruling élites have been worried that social order might be upset from below: whether it has been the fear of southern European immigration to the US at the beginning of the twentieth century or worries about welfare spending on an underclass at its end, the idea that social stratification might reflect underlying biological inequalities is without doubt a powerful ideological weapon.

Those who have been wary of biological determinisms have, however, often done so in the name of an exclusive freedom, as if any concession to the possibility of genetic predispositions to behaviour is *ipso facto* a loss of humanity. While they have rightly been critical of genetic essentialism, the idea that a person's 'true' identity is to be found in their DNA, they have leant towards its dialectical opposite, namely that a person's true identity is to be found in the ways that they have transcended their genetic inheritance. In the name of escape from genetic fate, many critics of genetic determinism have located true humanity in freedom from biology. In doing so, however, while they are right to reject certain misunderstandings of the role of genetics in behaviour, they also share in the same dualist frame of thought that we discussed in the previous chapter, one which identifies the self in opposition to the body.[9]

This raises the general theological problems which we discussed in the last chapter about separation of self from the body and the denial of the resurrection body that is implicit in dreams of releasing human beings from bodily frailty. In relation to genetic engineering these theological difficulties were connected with worries that the enhancement mentality would lead to an attitude that repudiated the possibility of tragedy and resisted the task of finding meaning in suffering. Here also rejection of the body leads to a denial of reality. As I suggested then, one of the elements of human flourishing is an ability to embrace as part of ourselves those aspects which we might readily reject as other or alien.

In relation to behavioural genetics this requires noting what the earlier points against genetic fatalism were in danger of suppressing, namely that there are biological predispositions to particular behaviours. Even if they may require particular environments for traits to be manifested, they still remain bio-logically given predispositions to behaviour. The task is not to pretend these away, but to learn to recognise their existence and only then to consider how to respond. To take a relatively trivial example, if I am genetically liable to find smoking very difficult to give up, I would do well to bear that in mind before taking up smoking or at least before imagining that my efforts to give up will be quickly rewarded. The issue is one of learning to know and come to terms with ourselves, adapting our behaviour where possible and appropriate. For some that may also involve recognising that there are some unwanted conditions which are fully penetrant and will be expressed in perhaps all environments. One day, we hope, there will be a treatment for Huntingdon's disease, for example; but until that time, those who have it are still faced with the task of learning to live with their condition.

This is not, to repeat from earlier chapters, a reason for rejecting research into appropriate therapeutic measures. Nor is it, as we have just seen in this chapter, a reason for denying the central role played by environmental conditions secured by just social and economic policy measures. On the contrary, it is a reason for thinking that increased genetic knowledge can also be a means of increasing our freedom. But this freedom is not best understood as something simply opposed to our biological make-up. Rather, freedom is fundamentally a virtue, something which comes from learning to come to terms with who we are and then deciding how to respond. It is not an escape from our bodily limitations into an ethereal world of pure, unconditioned choice, but involves a process of increasing self-knowledge, which is likely to include awareness of our genetic inheritance.

The understanding of ourselves that is emerging from the new genetics should not therefore be seen as a threat to individual liberty. But there is another danger which it raises, in relation to society as a whole. It could be that accepting that different people will have different genetic endowments will lend itself to new forms of social inequality. We need therefore to think carefully about issues of distributive justice. In recent decades, in liberal democracies across the world a number of governments, with a range of nominal political allegiances, have emphasised the centrality of equality of opportunity. On the political right, this has derived from a rejection of equality of outcome, in the belief that individuals should be allowed to benefit from their talents and enterprise. But on the left also, equality of opportunity has been used as a rallying cry for attacking social hierarchy, traditional power structures and unfair patterns of wealth distribution. Yet while such a meritocratic emphasis (if pursued seriously and not as a guise for preserving certain unjust power relations) could in principle remove some basic forms of unfairness, it is also intrinsically hostile to community and mutuality. For it makes the accentuation of individual difference the fundamental ordering principle of society, and denies the responsibility each has for the other. Whereas traditional socialism had followed a profound strand in Christian social thinking in asserting, 'From each according to their ability, to each according to their need', equality of opportunity declares simply, 'To each according to their ability'.

Now, a central component in an individual's abilities is, of course, their genetic endowment. Indeed, under an idealised model of equality of opportunity, the only thing that would differentiate people's achievement would be precisely their genetic inheritance. Therefore in thinking about genetics and society it is a central question if acceptance of genetic difference and the inequalities of inheritance will be used to reinforce the superiority of some in relation to others, or if the genetically based talents of each will be used in service of the good of all. When thinking about the issues raised by *The Bell Curve*, for example, this is the fundamental moral context within which the debate should be set, whatever the truth about the influence of genetics on intelligence.

This brings us right back to the question of the two different kinds of society, with which I opened the chapter. While behavioural genetics initially appears to touch our liberal anxieties about autonomy, the profounder problems it raises are to do with distributive justice and the common good. Whether the increased understanding of human behaviour which is emerging from the new genetics will be used for good or ill turns centrally on the model of society and of human beings with which we choose to approach it.

Genetic testing and insurance

This issue about justice and community, which we reached from a discussion of behavioural genetics, is also the central question in what at first sight seems to be an entirely separate matter, namely the use of genetic test results by insurance companies.

Fears about how confidential genetic information might be used by insurers has been a recurrent concern ever since the genetic test for Huntington's disease first became available in the late 1980s. Particular anxiety has arisen about the possible creation of a 'genetic underclass' – people whose genetic status, even pre-symptomatically, would prevent them from obtaining insurance coverage. In the United Kingdom and other countries with national health service provision this has principally been a concern about life insurance, which is a widely used means of contributing towards the financial protection of dependants should a wage-earner die, as well as often being linked to mortgages for purchase of a home. In the United States, however, the issue is much sharper, since health coverage is provided through private insurance companies, and refusal of health insurance can have very serious consequences for an individual.

In order to understand the central questions posed by the new genetics for the insurance industry, we need to distinguish two different approaches to insurance provision, the 'mutuality' and 'solidarity' models.[10] The first of these is the model adopted by private insurance companies, and is based on what are called 'standard underwriting practices'. These turn on a central principle of *equity*, namely that policy-holders with the same expected risk of loss pay the same premiums for a given level of cover. Those with a higher expected risk than the average may be required to pay higher premiums for that level of cover, or indeed may be refused insurance altogether; while those with a lower expected risk of loss may be offered lower premiums (at least by some insurance companies in some countries), a process known as 'cherry-picking'. Insurers are expected to discriminate between risks on the grounds that policy-holders may fairly be required to shoulder the risks of people in the same risk categories as themselves, but not of people who are more likely to make insurance claims.

The principle of equity is compromised under circumstances of what is known as 'adverse selection'. This can happen if, for example, someone withholds information about themselves relevant to possible future claims, or if insurers are not entitled to obtain information which is relevant to classifying risk properly. If this happens too much, or if insurers fail to classify risk properly for other reasons, an upward spiral of premiums can occur, since insurance companies will need to charge policy-holders more in order to pay out the claims being made. This can make that insurer uncompetitive, with the result that people transfer their business to other companies; or if it happens across the board, people may decide to leave the insurance market altogether.

Public insurance, by contrast, operates on the solidarity

model; this is the approach adopted in the UK by the National Health Service, for example, and is intended to ensure that everybody has a share in the benefits, regardless of their contribution. Central to this model is the principle of *equality*, that everybody is charged the same (or in accordance with their ability to pay), without regard to any expected risk of loss. Consequently there is no need to evaluate risk, and nobody is excluded because of a perceived high-risk status. Participation in solidarity schemes is typically compulsory, with contributions collected through the tax system. Moreover, there is no direct connection between an individual's contribution and the amount of benefit they may expect to receive. Because there are no options regarding level of payout, and nobody can gain unfairly at the expense of others through withholding information, solidarity schemes have no problems of adverse selection.

The dispute over genetic testing and insurance has arisen in relation to commercial, mutuality-based insurance. On the one hand, insurers argue that it is wrong for relevant health-related information to be withheld from them. If the principle of equity is fair, that individuals purchasing insurance should pay premiums in line with their perceived risk, it seems only right that those who are at risk from genetic diseases should be liable to pay higher premiums. (Within the terms of standard underwriting practices this would be known as 'acceptable discrimination'; it would only be unacceptable discrimination if the premiums were so high that they were disproportionate to the increased risks undertaken by the company.) Moreover, if those with genetic conditions ought to be paying more, it seems reasonable that the relevant information should be available to the insurance company. Otherwise it is unfair on the insurer – and on other policy-holders who may have to pay higher premiums – just as it is unfair if someone lies on their insurance application about their smoking habit. Genetic information should not be regarded as intrinsically different from any other kind of health-related information already required before a company decides whether to offer insurance.

Those on the other side, however, point to the threat that those who have a genetic condition, conceivably even without being aware of it, will be refused insurance, and as a result may not be able to provide for their dependants in case of death, may be refused a mortgage, or (in the US) may be denied private health cover altogether. For them, the development of new tests for different genetic diseases could turn out to be disastrous. While early talk of a genetically uninsurable under-class was dismissed in official responses, it remains the case that in many countries, including the US and UK, not nearly enough has yet been done to allay these fears.

Inevitably a certain amount of discussion turns on relatively detailed questions which there is not space in this book to address, such as the accuracy of particular genetic tests or the relative efficacy of different approaches to regulation of the insurance industry. But it is worth reviewing some of the general kinds of possible solution to the overall problem. One approach would be for governments to require commercial health insurers to provide coverage at lower than equitable rates for those who were liable to genetic disease. This may not be far in practice from what in fact is happening in some countries and some US states, namely a simple ban on using any genetic information in assessing insurance applications. A second possibility would be to require any relevant information that bears on categorisation of risk to be made available; inevitably this is favoured by many insurance companies, though not all of them. A third approach would mediate between these two, allowing insurers to use some information from genetic tests, but not all.[11]

Insurance companies are unhappy with the first approach, for reasons which we touched on earlier. It would make it more expensive for ordinary policy-holders at standard risks; this would make insurance in general less affordable, making it less attractive to people as a whole as well as less desirable for companies to be in insurance. Yet there are questions about this. For example, there is some evidence that insurers would not face as great an increase in costs as they might expect: some large insurers do not require disclosure of the results of genetic tests, which suggests that they at least do not think the extra costs are too great.[12] To take one instance, there are only about 200 new cases of Huntingdon's disease diagnosed in the UK each year, and not all of them are likely to have chosen the same insurer. Moreover, only late-onset diseases would lead to adverse selection, since early-onset diseases (which emerge in childhood or adolescence) would be diagnosed before insurance could have been applied for. And if necessary insurers could refuse to give insurance above a certain level unless the results of any genetic tests had been disclosed, or they could return a part of a policy-holder's contributions if they survived to term. In other words, there are ways of addressing the problem through imaginative development of new insurance products, which would not lead to the feared meltdown of the entire industry.

On the other hand, the consequences outside the insurance industry of requiring disclosure of test results could be very serious. For individuals, there is a serious danger of people refusing to take genetic tests for fear of compromising insurance applications, but thereby forfeiting the chance to receive early treatment they might benefit from. In terms of the likely success of treatment, this can be decisive in a number of cases, including breast and colon cancer. Medical research also suffers, since people are reluctant to participate in trials if these involve tests which count for insurance purposes. The public interest argument against requiring disclosure of genetic test results is very strong.

These considerations point towards some version of the second approach: at least a moratorium, and perhaps an outright ban. But there are wider issues as well. In many parts of the world, and certainly in the UK, the political pressure in the last decade and more has been towards placing the cost of healthcare and allied services on individuals, in an attempt to reduce governmental spending on welfare. This is augmenting the role played by private insurance companies, but it is inevitably also placing in an increasingly vulnerable position those who, for any reason, are unable to gain insurance. As commercial insurers jockey for advantage in an ever more competitive market, it becomes increasingly tempting to squeeze at the margins – perhaps through cherry-picking and offers of 'preferred life' terms to those with lower-than-average risks, or through more punitive terms or even refusal of insurance to those whose health risks can in any way be determined to be above average. And so they are quick to argue that genetic information is no different in principle from details about family history and other information which insurers routinely request.

Yet it cannot be blithely assumed that genetic information is no different from other information, as the social history of genetics, which we discussed in Chapter Three, makes clear.[13] And there are problems of a more general kind. Health risks are not best viewed as individual assets, but as collective burdens.[14] Genetic endowments which carry a higher-than-average level of health risk are not simply burdens which must be borne by individuals without respite from others. In allocating healthcare and related entitlements, it is not a proper ground for discrimination against someone that they have a particular health-related genetic heritage, any more than that they have a genetic endowment that leads to their being female or black. Any increased risk associated with genetic background is therefore something which in principle should be borne by society as a whole: this implies that it is ultimately the task of the state to ensure that there is no genetically uninsurable underclass. Whether the state chooses to do that by direct public provision for those who cannot obtain insurance from private providers, or by applying inducements to the private sector to allow everyone to be offered insurance on reasonable terms, is a secondary matter of implementation.

The emphasis on mutuality-based approaches to insurance creates a misleading moral picture. It suggests that insurance is fundamentally a matter of individuals managing risk prudently, rather than being a socially prescribed instrument for providing people with access to the services they need – certainly health care, but also adequate protection for dependants, including housing, and so on. The correct picture is one of the community as a whole assisting its members in the management of these burdens (in terms of the New Testament church community, this is cast in the vocabulary of bearing each other's burdens, visiting the sick, supporting orphans and widows in their distress, and so on). Subordinate to that goal, and oriented to it, there may be a role for private organisations to provide insurance, but they do so because the community as a whole decides that this would be an effective way of pursuing the common good. This is not to say that there should be no private insurance companies, which would require a much wider set of considerations; but it is to say that insurance companies are there for common benefit. Mutuality, at least in the insurance use of the term, must always be subordinate to solidarity.

Patenting of genes

While there may be a role for private enterprise, this discussion suggests, it can never be separated from the requirements of the common good. The same theme is central to a third problematic subject that has arisen out of the new genetics, namely the patenting of genes and genetic material. Here too, the fundamental issue is the relation of individual (or corporate) rights and the common good, though here there is also involved the nature of property rights. Even the question of whether life is something which may properly be patented resolves, as we shall see, into issues about the orientation of property to the good of all.

The debate over the patenting of genes has arisen out of the rush to gain control over the genetic information that has poured out of the Human Genome Project and other programmes involved in sequencing and mapping the human genome. By isolating and patenting genetic sequences, biotechnology companies, universities and similar bodies have been laying exclusive claims to the potentially massive financial returns that may accrue if successful therapies can be developed

from them. Similar claims are being staked on DNA stretches
in a whole variety of organisms, from crops such as rice, maize,
potatoes and wheat, through farm animals such as pigs, sheep,
and cattle, to less obvious examples such as spiders, barnacles
and the HIV virus. This activity is all happening at a spectacular
rate: at the time of writing patents were being taken out at
the rate of about 34,500 a month on different parts of the human
genome alone. Inevitably it has created fears. Will powerful
biotech corporations have a stranglehold on the development
of new gene-based therapies? Will the wealthy West – the vast
majority of patent-holders are from the US, western Europe
and Japan – use it as another means of exploiting developing
countries? Is 'life itself' now under the control of privately
owned commercial companies?

To address these questions, we should ask first why we have
a patents system at all. Patents were originally developed for a
variety of reasons. By ensuring that inventors and their in-
vestors would have exclusive claim for a period of time to the
profits from inventions, patents were intended to encourage
innovation, to allow people to benefit from their imagination,
inventiveness, and labour, and to encourage investment in risky
enterprises. A patent is therefore a form of time-limited intellectual property right, granted in exchange for public disclosure
of the knowledge patented (the word etymologically means a
'laying open', ironically in view of the fact that taking out
a patent can seem in the current climate more like a cornering
than a revealing of knowledge).

In order to be eligible for a patent, an invention must meet
certain criteria. While these vary slightly in wording from
country to country, they have three main elements: novelty,
utility and non-obviousness. To be novel, an invention must
not have been known and available to the public at the time of
the application. To have utility, a proposed patent must specify
concrete function, service, or purpose: it must be of beneficial
use to practical human activity. To be non-obvious, it must have
involved some inventive step that would not have been obvious
to someone skilled in the relevant field.

If there were no patent system, its defenders would say, the financial incentive to invent would not be present, which would mean the loss of a significant motor of enterprise. Of course, for many research scientists, particularly those working in health-related fields, other motives may well be more powerful (as well as worthier): pride in achievement, the satisfaction of having contributed to the conquest of disease, and so on. But in all privately funded research, as carried out by the biotech and pharmaceutical corporations, for example, scientists will not obtain financial investment for their projects unless other people are motivated by the hope of financial return, or at least by the expectation of reward in exchange for financial risk. And that in practice requires having a system of protecting the profits to allow companies to recoup their investments. Not allowing patents would result in a drastic loss of investment in new products, including in this case new drugs and other diagnostic and therapeutic techniques. Short of a massive economic restructuring, there is a strong prima facie case for supporting a patent system.

So what, if anything, is wrong with patenting human genetic material? A number of objections have been raised. Some are concerned about the unfairness of individuals or private corporations and their shareholders making large profits from knowledge about the genome which was initially obtained through the work of institutions funded either publicly or from large charitable foundations. This has been a particular issue in relation to the Human Genome Project. Much of the HGP's research was done by laboratories funded by the US and other governments or by foundations such as the Wellcome Trust in the UK. But in a celebrated dispute, the US-based company Celera Genomics, which had also made large contributions to sequencing the genome in the latter stages of the project, initially threatened to keep its data private with a view to generating income from it. In the event the threat did not materialise in precisely this form, largely as a result of a joint intervention by President Bill Clinton and Prime Minister Tony Blair calling for genomic data to be in the public domain. But it still remains the case that private companies stand to make money out of public largesse.

A second claim against gene patenting is that it represents a corruption of the patenting system. Fundamental to the notion of a patent is the distinction between a discovery and an invention. A feature of the natural world which is discovered cannot be patented: Watson and Crick could not have patented the helical structure of DNA, for example, any more than Roentgen could have patented X-rays (though, as a separate matter, they were all in a position to put a copyright on articles in which they published their discoveries). Historically, physical phenomena and products of nature were regarded as unpatentable. However, in a landmark decision in 1980, in the case of *Diamond v. Chakrabarty*, the US Supreme Court ruled that a genetically modified strain of bacteria which was designed to clear up oilspills could be patented. In doing so, it affirmed the historical principle that phenomena of nature in their natural state are not patentable, but added a major exception: goods that have been transformed from their natural state through human intervention. As a result patents began to be taken out on a variety of genetically engineered organisms and animals, including in 1988 the renowned Harvard 'oncomouse', which had been engineered to be susceptible to human breast cancer.

On this legal basis, therefore, genes are being patented. But, whatever its legal status, it is not clear that it is a rationally defensible position. Defenders of patenting claim that the process of isolating and purifying DNA is sufficient to justify its novelty. They also argue that describing gene function is non-obvious, and that providing descriptions of potential diagnostic and therapeutic functions of genes is demonstrating their utility. However, against this there is room for scepticism, although many of the relevant issues are technical. First, the process of isolating and purifying chemical elements, which in many cases is not a straightforward matter, has not been sufficient to justify patents on those elements: a patent application for tungsten, which had used this argument, failed in the US on the grounds that it was a product of nature. It is not at all clear that DNA sequences themselves (as opposed to the processes involved in isolating and purifying them) should properly be regarded as having been invented rather than discovered.[15] Second, most claims about the diagnostic and therapeutic uses of genes or gene sequences have not been demonstrated, but are speculative or at best exaggerated. At any rate, there is little that is as yet industrially applicable about them. And there is certainly nothing to justify the current practice of allowing the patent to apply not just to those uses of a gene specified in the patent, but also to all *potential* uses, even if they are as yet undiscovered.

A third argument against gene patenting is that the inadequacy of these controls on issuing patents on genes could ironically also end up stifling innovation, rather than encouraging it. Those who benefit financially turn out to be those who have done the routine work on DNA sequencing and mapping, rather than those who have made the decisive contributions in developing new drugs and the like. Patent-holders on genetic sequences, not having first demonstrated any serious medical application for their patented materials, may not be the people best equipped to explore the possibilities contained in them. Indeed, they may inhibit research, holding patents to more gene sequences than they are able to develop themselves, and charging those who might be more competent to make something of them. Medical researchers may face the task of jumping several hurdles, paying licence fees to multiple patent-holders, before they can work on the drugs and therapies which are the rationale for gaining the genetic knowledge in the first place. It would surely be better for pharmaceutical companies (which need not, of course, be different from biotech companies) to patent drugs and other diagnostic and therapeutic techniques that derived from genetic knowledge, rather than for the genes themselves to be patented.

But none of these arguments, for all their strength, address what many see as the central problem with gene patenting, namely that it is patenting *life*. To be sure, such critics accept, it is not patenting *a* life, a living human being, which would be tantamount to a kind of slavery, but it is staking a claim on something so intimate to human existence that it ought to be regarded as intrinsically beyond patenting. Of itself DNA may in one sense be no more than a complex molecule, but it is the chemical compound which is characteristic of living beings, and for this reason it should be given a special status that distinguishes it from other naturally occurring substances. Some would go further and argue that it is in fact gnostic (in the sense of evading the materiality of the body, as I discussed in the previous chapter) to deny any special value to DNA: it would be a denial of the biological given of human existence.

If one accepts the earlier argument that no product of nature may be patented and that DNA is in the relevant sense a product of nature, it follows that DNA ought not to be patented, regardless of the value one attributes to it. But *even* if one were to accept the *Chakrabarty* reasoning, there might still be good grounds for refusing to apply it to DNA. This can be seen by asking the question of what ontological status DNA should have. On the one hand, it is clearly not the same as a living organism, and certainly could not be regarded as having the value of a living human being. Patenting animals such as the oncomouse would on the face of it require greater justification than merely patenting DNA, since they have an ontological integration and identity which is of a different order than this complex molecule. And it is arguable that DNA cannot be regarded as being as important as bodily organs, for a similar kind of reason. It does not obviously have as high a status as living beings or body parts, therefore. On the other hand, this does not mean that it should be regarded as simply another naturally occurring chemical, with no special status. There seems something reductionist about denying DNA any special significance, given the role it plays in living beings. Life does have a distinct status in the Bible: while this is probably more a respect for the lives of creatures than a vitalist preoccupation with biological life as such, some respect for DNA might be an appropriate way of honouring this. In other words, it would be possible to recognise the significance of DNA, without this

leaning towards any kind of DNA mysticism or a genetic essen-
tialist assumption that DNA has a dominant or exclusive claim
on human identity. It would also mark a symbolic boundary
against the trend towards a commodification of life that many
rightly fear could result from the increasing commercialisation
of the life sciences.

What would such a special status mean in practice? It would
not prevent experimentation or research on DNA, or treating it
for daily laboratory purposes as just another chemical. But
it might justify treating it as being beyond patenting control.
Something like this is recognised in the Universal Declaration
on the Human Genome and Human Rights, adopted by the
United Nations in 1998, in its statement that 'The human
genome underlies the fundamental unity of all members of the
human family, as well as the recognition of their inherent
dignity and diversity. In a symbolic sense, it is the heritage of
humanity.' While this does not directly address the question
of patenting, it captures the sense that there is something intrinsically public about the human genome. Human DNA, in other
words, is properly regarded as part of our common human
heritage. This may carry the implication that individuals have
only limited rights over their genetic material if it has been
removed from their body with their consent; it may be that
someone who has a particularly interesting or rare allele is
not automatically entitled to profit from any therapies that are
derived from it. But it also implies that no corporation is entitled
to benefit from lucrative patents on that genetic sequence either.

Should we permit the patenting of genes, then? The arguments I have given above suggest not. There is a danger that the
practice has eroded or at least obscured the difference between
discovery and invention. It is not clear that the balance is in
favour of its fostering rather than stifling the development of
new medical treatments. The unique role the genome plays in
human identity suggests that it ought to be respected as part
of our common heritage, and this would be most appropriately
preserved through refusing to allow the patenting of gene
sequences. Much more appropriate would be the idea, sug-

gested by the biotechnology commentator Jeremy Rifkin, of a global treaty which would make the human gene pool an asset held in common and jointly administered by all nations on behalf of all future generations.[16] This would not prevent the patenting of specific *applications* of genetic knowledge by, say, pharmaceutical companies, which is a completely different matter. Here there is a much stronger case for a system of patents to ensure investment in research on new medicines – though we should never, of course, forget that these have been punitively exploited by many pharmaceutical companies in their efforts to prevent developing countries from obtaining the cheap drugs they need to address desperate health needs.

Needless to say, patenting of genes has been happening for a good while, and the financial pressures to continue the practice mean that it is not likely to be given up quickly. This implies that for now practical engagement in issues of gene patenting may have to address other issues: ensuring that an ethical dimension is introduced into the process of patent approval, and that this ethical criterion can be monitored and regulated effectively; returning discussions about intellectual property rights in genetic material and related things to the public realm, in recognition that patent offices are not best suited to enabling public discussion in such controversial areas; pressing for patent laws to be changed to meet some of the objections – for example, by allowing patents which relate only to specified uses of a gene, not *any* use; and so on. But it also implies a fundamental questioning of the way in which the pressures of a competitive commercial environment relentlessly work to absorb the common human inheritance into private hands. Private property is to be subordinated to the public good, and not vice versa.

Global justice

All three topics which we have discussed – behavioural genetics, genetic tests and insurance, and gene patenting – have

turned on strikingly similar issues. Despite the obvious differences in the wider concerns they have raised, each has been
connected with the orientation of the private to the public.
Developments in behavioural genetics have shown the importance of ensuring that differences in genetic endowments are
not used to reinforce the superiority of some over others. The
dangers of a genetically uninsurable underclass have made
clear the responsibility of government, as guardian of the
common good, either to require private insurers to ignore
genetic status in offering insurance, or to act as insurer of last
resort. And gene patenting has shown both the clear desirability
of preserving certain items as common, and the need for the
private intellectual property of patents to be subordinated to
the public good. In each case they have also shown the first
view of society that I discussed at the beginning of the chapter,
for which individual autonomy is the key, to be the path of
temptation, even if it is also the direction in which economic,
financial and legal structures in Western countries naturally
tend. By contrast, they have also shown the possibilities of the
second view, which sets individual and corporate freedom in
the context of wider social commitments.

The two pictures of society are also applicable at a global level
as well. A globalising world economy carries with it globalising
moral responsibilities. Once it is recognised that a nation's
responsibilities are not limited to the good of its citizens, but
also carry over its borders, a much broader perspective opens
up. For example, in relation to spending on health-care research,
the enormous disparity between resources devoted to the diseases of rich countries and those devoted to poor countries
becomes shocking: of the 56 billion US dollars spent annually
on medical research, 90 per cent is devoted to diseases causing
10 per cent of the global burden of disease.[17] The ruthless
pursuit of excessive profit has led pharmaceutical companies
to sue countries such as South Africa or Brazil for manufac-
turing or wishing to import cheaper generic drugs for AIDS,
despite their desperate public health situations: rarely can the
drive for profit have been placed above the needs of people so

graphically. Unless corporations begin to realise that they have responsibilities which lie beyond shareholder value, there is no reason to think that the same merciless logic of power will not be applied with newer genetic treatments as it has been with conventional drugs.

What stake does the church have in the second picture of society? It is precisely because we ask about the church that the answer becomes clear. Christian ethics is not in the first place about the decisions of individuals, but the witness of a community. That community is one in which people are called to carry each other's burdens, to share their possessions, to lay down their lives for each other, to grow in love. Individuals are important, of course: the good shepherd leaves the ninety-nine to search out the lost one. But it is precisely the one who is lost, who is marginalised, that is of concern: love for all requires special love for those most in need. As the church is called to model such relationships in its own life, so it in turn will call for such relationships to be replicated in wider society. Some further dimensions of this will be considered in the next chapter, when we look at the witness of such a community as a response to the spectre of runaway technology.

chapter five

Technological Inevitability and Alternative Futures

What futures can we imagine for genetic technology? How do they come out of the past? This chapter looks at the mentality of technology, and asks whether it is possible for the church to embody an alternative future.

THE YEAR IS 2350. A secret, high-level commission reports to the Health and Human Services Secretary in Washington DC on their findings. Developments in genetic enhancement technology, the eminent academics have concluded, are leading inexorably to a situation that had often been predicted by alarmists but had never been taken seriously by policy-makers. Genetic modifications had been routinely available for three hundred years, after some decades of initial research. At first they had been largely confined to replacing genes for obvious disorders, but pretty quickly enhancements for various athletic and cognitive traits had come on the market, as it was argued that distinctions between gene therapy and gene enhancement were fundamentally arbitrary. Those who were sufficiently wealthy had increasingly taken the use of genetic improvements for granted as part of giving their children a good start in life. Over time a class of people began to be identified who had benefited from several generations of genomic enhancements, and who typically married people of the same class and had children with them. A new biologically based class system had evolved. Despite the obvious new inequities that had arisen, no one had been able to stop the process. The right to reproduce using whatever means individuals could afford had long been accepted as fundamental to their way of life. The corporations which had researched, produced and marketed the procedures collectively accounted for a large part of the American economy. Other countries had banned the use of genetic enhancements, and had suffered economically as a result. Politicians, business leaders and opinion-formers in the media and the universities were all from the genetically enriched class, as were those at the forefront of every area of society; inevitably they were reluctant to make changes which would call things into question too radically. Those who had not benefited from generations of engineering had rarely managed to achieve positions of power, and were too disunited and distracted by other concerns to mount any effective protest about the situation, beyond some occasional rioting.

The alarming new situation described in the secret government report suggested that by the end of the third millennium the growing division between the two classes would lead to sharply decreased fertility rates whenever a genetically enriched person attempted to have children with a 'natural'. The implication was stark: as the report put it, there would be 'entirely separate species with no ability to cross-breed, and with as much romantic interest in each other as a current human would have for a chimpanzee'. It was not clear how this result could be avoided. Even if the political will were there for it to be banned in the US, biotechnology companies and their customers would simply move to poorer countries that needed the revenue. Moral appeals to the enhanced class would probably not work either: given that it was in each individual's interests to continue to give their children a better genetic inheritance, and nobody was being directly or clearly harmed by their actions, it was going to be virtually impossible to persuade more than a few to change their behaviour. The free choices of individuals had inexorably led to a situation that could not be regarded as best for the population as a whole.

This imaginary scenario is taken from the epilogue to a recent book on human genetics by Lee Silver, a professor of molecular biology at Princeton.[1] What is interesting about it – and many like it, from H. G. Wells (who was the inspiration for ideas about the division of the human species) onwards – is not so much the details of what is predicted as happening in the future, temporarily diverting though these may be. Rather, it is the way in which they project the future as a sequence of events that have a certain inevitability about them. Of course, much science fiction is written entirely as futuristic fantasy, with no connections to the present world, whether explicit or implicit. But many of the best writings in the genre have risen to prominence precisely because of their ability to express in fictional form both the desires and fears of contemporary society, and its underlying social and technological trends. In describing an imaginary future world, they manage both to reflect our aspirations and anxieties, and to show how, in conjunction with technological advance, these might generate a society at once like our own and yet hauntingly different from it.

The question, of course, is how a vision such as this merely explores our fears about the future, and how much it is a potentially serious account that extrapolates from current developments. It would, of course, be easy to write the scenario off as mere science fantasy. But part of its fascination is precisely that it draws on attitudes, commitments and trends with which we are well familiar, and in doing so manages to articulate a disturbing sense of their inevitability. Whether it is justified or not, this feeling of an unavoidable future lurks in the cultural imagination, such that even those who are resolutely opposed to some of the potential developments in genetics are resigned to the belief that they are going to happen anyway. Pressure-group activists and religious moralists, culture critics and tabloid editors, all may reject genetic engineering, but they do so with the sense that the tide of history is against them.

It is this sense of technological necessity which I wish to explore in this final chapter. Are developments towards a genetically engineered future inevitable, or are they contingent?

Is it possible for us to tell a different story about our future, or are we somehow irredeemably caught in the slipstream of runaway technology? These take up questions which we raised in Chapter Two when discussing the dangers of commodifying children, in Chapter Three when considering trends towards a new eugenics, and in Chapter Four when contrasting two different kinds of society. All of these relate to different visions of the future and, in Christian terms, to different eschatologies, different understandings of how history will be fulfilled in Christ.

The Baconian project

To answer these questions we need to have a deeper sense of some of the fundamental forces which are generating modern technological medicine. Too often ethics, both theological and philosophical, proceeds as if all that is needed for a sufficient response to these genetic developments is an understanding of the moral principles or correct ethical method which should be applied to them. But this kind of applicationist approach runs the danger of ignoring deeper social and cultural trends: it neglects the underlying patterns of thought and practice which have given rise to the relatively superficial phenomena of particular technologies such as genetic manipulation.

Ethical analyses which only attend to the presenting issues of each emerging new technology will not finally understand any such technology in its entirety. Because they do not appreciate the underlying cultural flow, they are doomed to be reactive, only capable of responding when the next moral crisis over a new technology erupts. What is needed instead is an understanding of the cultural dynamic which both creates the new technologies and shapes the ways in which contemporary societies characteristically respond to them. That is, we need an account of the broader historical and cultural shifts which can set in context particular developments in reproductive and genetic technologies. Only then will we avoid a continued sense of bewildered shock as the seemingly unstoppable juggernaut of technology rolls on.

I want to start on this exercise by drawing on the account of modern technological medicine given by Gerald McKenny in his book, *To Relieve the Human Condition*.[2] McKenny traces the roots of modern medicine to what he calls 'the Baconian project', named after the British philosopher Francis Bacon (1561–1626). This project has centred on two imperatives: the elimination of suffering, and the expansion of the realm of human choice. Its origins lay in the wake of the Reformation. Protestant Christianity emphasised that justification was received through faith, and was not obtained through continual religious observance or devotional practice. It turned people's attention away from such efforts to secure eternal life, towards everyday concerns for the well-being of their neighbour. This worldly service became central, and in turn encouraged the search for ways of making practical benevolence more effective.

As a result of the influence of Francis Bacon and others of his time, these efforts increasingly were thought to require an instrumentalisation of the natural world, treating it as mere passive raw material to be used for whatever human purposes could be devised. Importantly for the future of medicine, the natural world that could be manipulated in this way increasingly came to include the human body. The new science of the seventeenth century also assisted in this: this overthrew the classical teleological account of nature, understanding it instead as an inert mechanism which could be explained solely in terms of efficient causes – hence the clockwork and mechanical metaphors which characterised scientific understanding of the physical world for some centuries afterwards. Nature could become an object of control, and so could be bent to its proper purpose of glorifying God and benefiting human beings.

The radical Enlightenment in the eighteenth century took further the project of practical compassion. The early utilitarians of the time calculated the good of the neighbour by identifying it with the maximisation of the neighbour's pleasure and the minimisation of their pain. While later utilitarians were to interpret happiness and the human good in less crude ways than this, the ideal of the relief of suffering became central to modern culture; and the ability to contribute to such relief has remained one of the principal criteria by which any institution or system of thought, whether religious or secular, is judged. At the same time, the new scientific understanding of nature as a closed system brought into question the notion of divine providence, replacing it instead with the deist idea of an absent God. This required a new interpretation of suffering: no longer was there any point in trying to discern God's hand in suffering, or in seeing it as a means of spiritual growth. It was now basically meaningless, something to be avoided or eliminated wherever possible. And, of course, the technological power over nature which the new science had made available was well suited to making a contribution to this. Providence was coming to be understood as arbitrary fate, and technological science working through medicine was beginning to take on the quasi-salvific role of helping people to escape it.

The value of individual autonomy also started to become important for medicine. This ideal, which was mediated to the late eighteenth- and nineteenth-century world through the Romantics, emphasised the role of individual consent in relation to medical intervention. The growth of medical control over the body as a result increasingly had to take account of an individual's preferences in relation to their body. While it might only be by the late twentieth century that the principle of informed consent became widely acknowledged in medical practice, the foundations for it had been laid much earlier. And just as the notion of consent in general has more recently turned into an emphasis on active choice and the ideal of self-determination, so consent to medical interventions in the body is now steadily turning into the instrumental use of medical intervention to achieve a range of individually defined consumer choices over one's body. As McKenny puts it, 'the commitment to eliminate all suffering combined with an imperative to realize one's uniqueness leads to cultural expectations that medicine should eliminate whatever anyone might consider to be a burden of finitude or to provide whatever anyone might require for one's natural fulfilment.'[3]

The Baconian project is not only a programme of practical change, with a commitment to everyday benevolence and the relief of suffering and a concomitant recasting of nature, providence, the relation of the self to the body, and so on. It has also moulded ethics in its own shape. Anything which questions the nature-transcending account of medicine becomes morally unintelligible. Far from maintaining a critical distance, which might allow it at least in principle to question any activity connected with the body, standard modern bioethics is entirely complicit with the commitments to personal liberty, technological control, and relief from actual or potential suffering which comprise the Baconian project. Any alternative view of medicine, which asks not how medicine can be subordinated to the desire to transcend the frailties of human existence, but how sickness and health can be integrated into a morally valuable life that has come to terms with the limitations of finitude and mortality, is dismissed or misrepresented. Standard bioethical theories are largely variations on Kantian or utilitarian themes, but the disputes between them are relatively parochial. They both share in a broader allegiance to the instrumentalisation of nature and the alienation of the self from the body which marks them out as true heirs of the Baconian project. As a consequence, if that project is to be radically questioned, it is unlikely to be in terms supplied by conventional bioethics.

A story such as this unavoidably simplifies a much more complex process of historical and intellectual change. But the dangers in this should not detract from the value of developing a broader perspective from which to view developments in modern medicine. Nor should we be put off this analysis of the Baconian project by certain other problems or misinterpretations. For example, accepting it does not imply a nostalgic search for a pre-modern golden age; to say that there are things wrong with the modern world is not the same as to wish to return to an earlier period of history, even though there may be things that can be learned from the past. Nor does it mean a rejection of all individual technologies that have emerged in recent times: it is quite compatible with the discerning effort to distinguish between those technological interventions which should be embraced and those which should be rejected. Perhaps most importantly, to be critical of the Baconian project does not mean that relieving suffering and exercising choice are bad goals. On the contrary, it recognises that they are good; indeed, it is precisely because they are good that it is so difficult to recognise that they can be distorted, and can become integral to ideals which are morally problematic.

But this kind of account is a powerful aid in helping us to understand many of the most characteristic features of modern medicine. For example, the Baconian emphasis on the use of technological means to control fate helps to explain the instinctive tendency to turn to technical means as therapy of first resort, as well as the marginalising of medical disorders which cannot, at this stage of medicine, be cured (such as mental illness) and of those medical professions which are concerned as much with caring as curing (such as nursing, traditionally understood). Its central commitment to eliminating suffering gives rise to the assumption that all suffering is pointless, and therefore that there is little value in attempting to find meaning in it. Its desire to rise above fate and to increase choice leads to an instrumentalisation of the body, and an increasing understanding of the body as manipulable in accordance with individual tastes and preferences.

The inevitability of genetic engineering

This description of the Baconian project also fills in a missing link in our understanding of the seeming inevitability of genetic engineering. In Chapter Three I argued that there are reasons for thinking that the kinds of forces which have led to the new eugenics of pre-natal screening and abortion are also likely to contribute to a drive towards genetic enhancement. I suggested that there are four desires which are at the heart of the pressures in that direction: the desire to have a child, the desire to have a child genetically related to oneself, the desire to have a healthy child, and – most importantly for this question – the desire to give one's child the best start in life. This last desire is likely over time to lead to demands that parents have rights to make choices not only in relation to the environment in which their children are brought up, but also to the genetic make-up which they receive in the first place.

I should make clear that none of these desires is in itself wrong. The problem is that they are understood and acted on in a way that makes genetic enhancements more likely. For a start, they are often constructed as natural. That is, in the culture as a whole they tend to be interpreted in a way which promotes conformity with them as a kind of accordance with one's deepest nature, and stigmatises those who reject them or understand them in culturally deviant ways. In our current climate this is reinforced by a genetic essentialism which associates personal identity, despite all its historical and social complexity, primarily with genetic make-up, and emphasises the perpetuation of an individual's genetic line as central to their personal fulfilment.[4]

Moreover, they are set in a particular social, economic and technological context. If the marketing of cosmetics and increasingly of aesthetic surgery is any indication, there is likely to be intense commercial attraction to research into and manufacture of cosmetic genetic enhancements, once issues of safety and reliability have been sorted out. Also the incentives for scientific research in the area are likely to remain high into the indefinite future; this is true whether the motives of individual scientists are 'good' (the putatively disinterested search for knowledge or the enjoyment of discovery or invention) or 'bad' (the desire for prestige or financial gain). The language of rights too may play an increasingly determinative role, as it increasingly becomes the instrument by which people defend their lifestyle preferences from the feelings of others. Thus in this case, the argument may go, people should of course not be obliged to choose genetic engineering for themselves or their children (though we saw reasons in Chapter Three for not taking for granted a right not to be genetically manipulated), but they should not force their disgust on others who might want it for themselves or their children. If individuals or couples want to choose this option, provided that nobody is evidently harmed, their right to privacy should be respected.

For these reasons and others, such as the increasing emphasis on 'responsible' reproduction that leaves nothing to chance, as well as the philosophical difficulties in drawing a clear line between therapy and enhancement, I suggested in Chapter Three that a creeping trend towards genetic enhancement is not implausible. But the Baconian project adds an extra dimension to these which reinforces their power. For it links all of these factors with a set of cultural themes centring on the elimination of suffering and the expansion of choice. And in doing so it gives them an existential aspect, a connection with another quality of motivation. This explanatory factor is arguably much less easy to discern for those who limit themselves to the standard explanatory categories of the sociological repertoire. But it is surely because the four desires are interpreted within the cultural context of the existential desire to be rid of suffering altogether that they have a peculiar power. The aspirations which they represent are deeply enough rooted as it is, but that they are set in this broader context only serves to emphasise that they have come to possess a nearly religious force. Genetic engineering seems fated to happen because it arises from the conjunction of two separable, albeit interconnected, movements: the features which characterise this particular technology, and those which characterise Baconian modernity as a whole.

It is wrong therefore to represent the technological drive towards genetic manipulation as an alien power, an external force which conspires against us despite our best intentions. It works right through the motions of our own psyches and gains its power from some of our deepest commitments. Indeed, it is tempting to think that the shrillness of our repudiations of genetic engineering may be an index of its closeness to our hearts. Its seeming inevitability may be a reflection of our bondage to particular desires for ourselves and our children, as well as our allegiance to technological manipulation as a means of salvation from blind fate.

This account is more substantial than a mere rhetorical appeal to slippery slopes. It contains, after all, a clear story about the causes that are leading towards genetic enhancement, and cannot be dismissed airily on the grounds that we cannot know the future. If it is to be rejected, a substantial argument is needed to show why these causal factors are not as important as it suggests, or why other ones should be given greater weight. It also makes evident why it may not be adequate to talk about simply deciding to tell ourselves different stories about the future, the possibility which was discussed in Chapter One in relation to Frankenstein. The fears about technological control over the body which that myth has articulated are too deep to be eliminated by straightforwardly elaborating alternative myths: the myth gains its potency in part precisely because it also represents a quite proper fear about being a creator, becoming as God. It is this existential, quasi-salvific dimension which is brought out by analysing these developments in terms of the Baconian project.

Towards an alternative

Is an alternative possible? One answer to this might be to point out all the contingencies in the narrative I have presented. That is, rather than assuming that genetic engineering is inevitable, one could demonstrate the many ways in which history does not turn out as predicted. For example, in this case, it would be reasonable to suspect that the scientific and technical problems may be much greater than the story admits. Scientists and their promoters may exaggerate the benefits or the speed with which they will be reaped out of naïvety, ignorance, or the desire to secure funding. In particular, issues of safety are likely to remain decisive in many areas of genetic intervention for perhaps decades to come: until we can be much clearer about the various consequences of replacing a particular gene, for example, moves towards positive genetic engineering are likely to remain limited. Time may also be a factor. Manipulation of fruit-flies or mice is easier, not least because the effects over several generations are soon apparent, whereas in the case of human beings the effects may not be clear literally for generations.

There are many other unknowns. Unpredictable historical turns of events – for example, a widespread popular reaction against globalisation, capitalism, technology and all things genetic – could slow developments down, as could restrictive employment of gene patents. Perhaps as compelling as any is the severe possibility that the combined pressure of global population growth and environmental degradation during the course of the twenty-first century may turn public attention so decisively away to other matters that spending money on genetic enhancement may come to be viewed as nothing other than obscene.

Yet, for all the ways in which the narrative can be deconstructed, it remains the case that our current expectations are firmly that history is moving in a particular direction. It is a necessary and valuable task to show that those expectations may be proved wrong, but this does nothing to call into question the causal factors which underlie them and which will continue to prove decisively influential if nothing else intervenes. By itself it is a negative and impotent exercise.

For Christian theology, what is rather at stake in thinking about the inevitability of certain developments within history is the nature of eschatology. The church is called into being to witness to a time when the reign of God and the redemption of the world will be manifest to all. This implies showing in this present time that the necessities of the world are not final, that there are real alternatives. Thus, if the form of sinning that is characteristic of the modern world can in part be described in terms of bondage to technological necessity, the church is called to witness to the liberation from these compulsions of our sinful nature that has been wrought through the death and resurrection of Jesus Christ. And this is not simply a matter of preaching, or of verbal denunciation of particular trends. Precisely because the Word became flesh and dwelt amongst us, and because the Holy Spirit – the Spirit of Christ – is with us until the end of the age, it is open for the church even now to begin to experience in its life some of the promised freedom. It is possible for the church in its life to show that there is an authentic alternative to technological necessities, that these are in the end no more than contingent features of a passing world.

What might this mean for the church in practice? Of course, it might be that the churches believe that in relation to genetics, things are in general terms going in a healthy direction. While there are certain undesirable side-effects, all that is needed is a little tinkering, a few adjustments to the machine: perhaps some more regulation here or there, a few pronouncements from synods, bishops, or boards of social responsibility, some more international declarations. No doubt such exercises are valuable. But by themselves they are in danger of reinscribing the traditional Christian responses to new developments in technology: first, hand-wringing, lamenting the complexity of the moral issues and the inability of our moral wisdom to keep up with our technical powers; and second, ambulance work, rushing to make a public response to the latest moral crisis as yet another scruple is run over by the juggernaut of technology.

None of these get to the heart of the issue. What is needed is the embodiment of a counter-narrative, a different story that shows the contingency of the dominant narrative. What might such an alternative narrative look like? I will start with the four desires which I have suggested are central to these developments in reproductive and genetic technology.

First, instead of the desire to have children, we should note the role played by celibacy in Christian thought. Not only has the choice not to have children been an intelligible option within Christianity, it has for large parts of Christian history been regarded as the preferred alternative, both reflecting the life of Jesus himself and witnessing to the possibility of single-minded devotedness to God and the cause of God's Kingdom.

Such an alternative has been seen in the Christian tradition as a divine calling, and it has equally opened up the possibility of interpreting the choice to be married and have children as a calling. But precisely because the decision whether or not to have children is interpreted within the context of discernment about what faithfulness to God involves, not only does it forestall any naturalistic interpretation of the desire to have children that might render them essential to personal fulfilment, it also prevents the decision whether or not to have them from being reduced to a self-gratifying lifestyle choice – and in doing so puts up a barrier to their becoming consumer items.

Second, instead of the desire to have children who are biologically related to oneself, it is open to Christians to construe the desire to have children in terms of the value of adoption. Christians can understand adoption not as a last-stop response to infertility when all else has failed, but as a positive choice to reflect in their lives the fact of having been adopted as children of God.

Third, instead of the desire to have a healthy child taking on the aura of necessity, such that all means may be employed to remove disability, Christians may recognise the centrality to the authentic life of the church of those who are disabled. Indeed, here perhaps more than anywhere we can see the alternative to the Baconian mentality. In the presence of those who are disabled, for whom medicine can find no cure, Christians find themselves stripped of false security, aware of the illusions and potential cruelty of human efforts to transcend finitude. Disability, as we saw in Chapter Three, is a reminder that none of us is all right. It is an invitation to all of us, whether or not we see ourselves as disabled, to enter on the journey of learning to embrace our common human fragility and our need for each other if we are to flourish.

Finally, instead of the desire to give one's child the best start in life, which too easily becomes translated into the competitive necessity of giving one's child a better start than anyone else's, Christians may find the source of their value in Christ. In doing so, they can be freed from the frenzied compulsions and insecurities which lead to placing inordinate demands both on themselves as providers for their children, and on their children who are required to perform in line with their expectations. There are limits to what parents can provide and what they can expect, and Christians have nothing to fear from not finding their identity in their children's achievements.

In each case what is criticised is not the desire itself: it is not wrong to want to have children, or to have children 'of one's own', or to have healthy children, or to give them the best start in life. What is criticised is the idea that the culturally prevalent understanding of how these desires should be fulfilled is essential to human happiness or the human good. In each case there are real alternatives, and these have been recognised as such in the Christian tradition. Of course, these alternatives cannot remain merely voiced ideals, but must be practically realisable as an everyday reality for those in the church – they are not, after all, real alternatives if nobody practises them. They are also necessarily a feature of the church as community. It is not possible in any straightforward way for an individual to witness both to the good of having children and to the good of not having children, for example: rather, as a community some will be called to exemplify some of these goods, some to exemplify others, while all are called to witness to the goodness of each other's callings.

Much more could be said to give substance to these responses to the four desires. We would need to avoid suggesting that celibacy is easy or that infertility does not hurt or that disability in one's child is never demanding. We would need to detail practical ways in which the church can act, and so on. Furthermore, the church has things to say and do about the other social and economic factors which I mentioned earlier as also decisively contributing to a climate that makes positive genetic engineering seem necessary: commercialism, consumerism, and the rest. But the main point is that there are practical ways of addressing the seeming necessity of positive genetic engineering. While they may not appear very closely connected to the technology, they do attempt to reach the fundamental motivations and structural forces which give rise to the sense of its inevitability.

But the church has an alternative not only to the forces which are contributing towards the apparent necessity of genetic engineering. It also has an alternative vision of the human good to that found in the Baconian project as a whole. While it may be this dimension which makes most evident the quasi-salvific aspect of genetic engineering, I have put this last to make clear that the church is not just about the 'existential' dimensions of life, the ultimate in abstraction from the penultimate: rather it is about the whole of life lived in such a way as to reveal the character and acts of God, about witnessing to the ultimate through the penultimate.

We can articulate the Christian counter-narrative to the understanding of the human good described in the Baconian project by reiterating some of the theological themes which have underlain the previous three chapters. For example, in response to the idea that life is at the whim of arbitrary fate, Christians understand it to be ruled by providence. Suffering therefore may at times need to be accepted, as something which is in principle capable of increasing our knowledge of God and of ourselves and our dependence on God. But to understand fate as providence is not just an intellectual commitment. It is also a virtue, acquired by the disciplined and steadfast effort involved in learning to look for hints of good where none is apparent. This requires learning how to reject the glib assertion that suffering is something other than suffering: pain hurts. But equally it means knowing how to refuse despair or the casting of blame onto an impersonal force such as 'life'.

Again, in relation to the value of individual autonomy, Christians should question any notion of choice which neglects the character of the chooser. While the Baconian view of the self leaves it vulnerable to being understood as simply a bundle of instincts or sub-rational desires, Christians should see persons as moral beings, growing in knowledge and understanding of the good, and being formed in the virtues that constitute such growth. Equally, they should be sceptical of any stress on autonomy which makes choice paramount, such that the content of what is chosen is totally eclipsed by celebration of the fact that it has been chosen: freedom to choose is without question valuable, but it is so in the context of its being oriented to choosing the good. Perhaps most importantly of all, Christians should reject the legitimation which the language of individual autonomy gives to the wealthy and powerful to ignore the needs of the poor and powerless.

Finally, in relation to the dualism of self and world which gives rise to the instrumentalisation of the body, Christians assert the life of the resurrection. Some of the aspirations which we have for our bodies, which modern medicine and genetics are being asked to fulfil, imply a growing dissociation of the self from the body. Instead of helping us to identify ourselves with our bodies, our culture increasingly sees the body as something which is to be transcended, to be manipulated in accordance with desire. One response to this is to call for an acknowledgement of our human limits and a recognition that we are better understood as body–soul unities. Of course, Christians also wish to affirm this. Yet as we saw in Chapter Three, the Christian response to efforts to transcend the body is rooted not in a chastened recollection of finitude, but in the hope of a decisive transformation of our bodies into the resurrection body. Transcendence of our bodily life is to be found not in escape from our physicality, but in the hope of our resurrection.

Conclusion

It could be argued that the church (or in empirical terms, particular church communities or groups of Christians) learning to respond in this way will not make much difference to the necessity of technology in the culture at large. After all, the scale of the problem is vast, and the church is small, divided and largely seduced by the technological promise. Yet, for Christians, social effectiveness should never be the primary criterion of the church's witness. This is a symbolic resistance, witnessing to the kind of life Christ makes possible, one which is learning to be freed from the compulsions and desires that make genetic engineering seem inevitable. That this resistance is symbolic indicates two things. On the one hand, the church's primary commitment is not to causal effectiveness, to being a successful agent of history. Rather its first task is to witness to the Kingdom, to point to the promise of a world made new. On the other, it indicates that the church genuinely participates in that to which it points. In its embodied and shared life, it is beginning to experience the reality of the Kingdom which it proclaims. In empirical sociological terms, such church communities being formed in this way may be small-scale. But such an exercise is not mere tokenism: it is an incarnate lifestyle which really does open out different possibilities in this world. Indeed, though it does not depend on public recognition for its identity, such a witness does not preclude the possibility of setting in train broader cultural resonances which might increasingly weight the options towards genuine choice about genetic engineering in the wider world.

The first task of the church, therefore, is not so much to 'make a contribution to the public debate' as to start living the difference. By being true to its deepest commitments, and by learning itself of its own narcissism and denial of reality, its own failures in justice and its desire for control, it could genuinely start to come to know and point to another story. In doing this, it might help the wider culture come to the kind of self-knowledge that is necessary to discern which genetic manipulations might be acceptable and which unacceptable, as I intimated at the end of Chapter Three. Of course, this does not mean that the church should say nothing in the public realm about any of these matters – though such declarations should be seen as secondary to the practical task of getting the church's own house in order.[5] But it does suggest that the self-knowledge which the wider culture gains might turn out to be the occasion for penitence as much as for self-congratulation. And if that were to happen, we might truly be able to look forward to the story of a more humane future.

Notes

Chapter 1: **Introduction**

1. James D. Watson, 'The Human Genome Project: Past, Present, and Future', *Science* 248, no. 4951 (6 April 1990), 44–9, at 44.
2. Leon Kass, 'The Wisdom of Repugnance', *The New Republic* (2 June 1997), reprinted in Gregory E. Pence (ed.), *Flesh of My Flesh: The Ethics of Cloning Humans: A Reader* (Lanham, Md.: Rowman & Littlefield, 1998), pp. 13–37. Cf. Mary Midgley, 'Biotechnology and Monstrosity: Why We Should Pay Attention to the "Yuk Factor" ', *Hastings Center Report* 30, no. 5 (2000), 7–15.
3. For an excellent account of the reception of the Frankenstein myth in popular culture, see Jon Turney, *Frankenstein's Footsteps: Science, Genetics and Popular Culture* (New Haven: Yale University Press, 1998).

Chapter 2: **Health, Medicine and the New Genetics**

1. See in general George Khushf, 'Illness, the Problem of Evil, and the Analogical Structure of Healing: On the Difference Christianity Makes in Bioethics', *Christian Bioethics* 1, no. 1 (1995), 102–20; reprinted in Stephen E. Lammers and Allen Verhey (eds), *On Moral Medicine: Theological Perspectives in Medical Ethics*, 2nd edn (Grand Rapids, Mi.: Eerdmans, 1998), pp. 30–41.
2. Ibid., p. 31.
3. Ibid., 34.
4. See David S. King, 'Preimplantation Genetic Diagnosis and the "New" Eugenics', *Journal of Medical Ethics* 25 (1999), 176–82, at 179.
5. Ted Peters, 'Cloning Shock: A Theological Reaction', in Ronald Cole-Turner, *Human Cloning: Religious Responses* (Louisville, Ky.: Westminster John Knox Press, 1997), pp. 12–24, at 23.
6. Human Genetics Advisory Commission and Human Fertilisation and Embryology Authority, *Cloning Issues in Reproduction, Science and Medicine* (January 1998), s. 3. The term 'therapeutic cloning' succeeded in alienating supporters and critics alike, the former alarmed that such an evidently beneficial procedure could be lumbered with the unfortunate overtones of cloning, the latter rejecting the idea that a process which destroyed embryos could be described as in any sense therapeutic. In the subsequent report it was changed to the rather less snappy 'Therapeutic Use of Cell Nucleus Replacement'.
7. Quoted in Timothy F. Murphy, 'Our Children, Our Selves: The Meaning of Cloning for Gay People', in Gregory E. Pence (ed.), *Flesh of My Flesh: The Ethics of Cloning Humans: A Reader* (Lanham, Md.: Rowman & Littlefield, 1998), pp. 141–9, at 142.
8. For these, and for other issues about reproductive technologies discussed in this paragraph, see the companion volume in this series by Brent Waters, *Reproductive Technologies: Towards a Theology of Procreative Stewardship* (London: Darton, Longman and Todd, 2001).

9. In relation to cloning as a means of producing offspring for gay people, it is not clear that gay and lesbian groups would have been so keen on cloning if they were able to benefit from other more traditional means of bearing children: as Timothy Murphy has argued, the initial enthusiasm for cloning is better seen as moral displacement, a way of drawing attention to the prejudices that currently exist against gay people adopting, fostering, and having legal rights to keep their own children ('Our Children, Our Selves', op. cit.). See also Karen Lebacqz, 'Genes, Justice and Clones', in Ronald Cole-Turner (ed.), *Human Cloning: Religious Responses* (Louisville, Ky.: Westminster John Knox Press, 1997), pp. 49–57.

10. Strictly this need not require cloning, i.e. transfer of a somatic cell nucleus, but only egg nuclear replacement, i.e. transfer of an egg nucleus.

11. Ronald M. Kline, 'Whose Blood Is It Anyway?', *Scientific American* 284, no. 4 (April 2001), 30–37.

12. For a good overview of the arguments in general for and against germ-line gene therapy, see LeRoy Walters and Julie Gage Palmer, *The Ethics of Human Gene Therapy* (New York: Oxford University Press, 1997), pp. 80–88.

13. Congregation for the Doctrine of the Faith, *Declaration on Procured Abortion* 13, in *Acta Apostolicae Sedis* 66 (1974), 739.

14. Germain Grisez, *The Way of the Lord Jesus*, vol. 2: *Living a Christian Life* (Quincy, Ill.: Franciscan Press, 1993), p. 496.

15. Norman M. Ford, *When Did I Begin? Conception of the Human Individual in History, Philosophy and Science* (Cambridge: Cambridge University Press, 1988).

16. Ibid., p. 136.

17. Helen Watt, *Life and Death in Healthcare Ethics* (London: Routledge, 2000), pp. 9–10.

18. On other versions of the developmentalist argument, see my 'Whose Sanctity of Life? Ricoeur, Dworkin and the Human Embryo', in Stephen Barton (ed.), *Holiness Past and Present* (Edinburgh: T. & T. Clark, forthcoming, 2002).

19. Helen Watt, *Life and Death in Healthcare Ethics*, pp. 61–2.

Chapter 3: **Genetic Enhancement and the New Eugenics**

1. Plato, *Republic*, 457b–461e.

2. Daniel Kevles, *In the Name of Eugenics: Genetics and the Uses of Human Heredity* (Cambridge, Ma.: Harvard University Press, 2nd edn, 1995), p. 3.

3. Ibid., pp. 96–112.

4. Ibid., pp. 114–15.

5. Diane Paul, *Controlling Human Heredity: 1865 to the Present* (Atlantic Heights, NY: Humanities Press, 1995), p. 86.

6. Kevles, *In the Name of Eugenics*, p. 116.

7. Paul, *Controlling Human Heredity*, pp. 121–5.

8. Dorothy Nelkin and M. Susan Lindee, *The DNA Mystique: The Gene as a Cultural Icon* (New York: W. H. Freeman, 1995), p. 31.

9. W. R. Inge, 'Eugenics', in *Outspoken Essays: Second Series* (London: Longmans, Green and Co., 1922), pp. 254–75, at 257.

10. For eugenics in the British churches, see Greta Jones, *Social Hygiene in Twentieth Century Britain* (London: Croom Helm, 1986), pp. 47–50.

11. Anne Kerr, Sarah Cunningham-Burley, and Amanda Amos, 'Eugenics and the New Genetics in Britain: Examining Contemporary Professionals' Accounts', *Science, Technology and Human Values* 23 (1998), 175–98.

12. Daniel Kevles, 'Eugenics and the Human Genome Project: Is the Past Prologue?', in Timothy F. Murphy and Marc A. Lappé (eds), *Justice and the*

Human Genome Project (Berkeley: University of California Press, 1994), pp. 21–2.

13. Cf. Tom Shakespeare, 'Losing the Plot? Medical and Activist Discourses of Contemporary Genetics and Disability', in Peter Conrad and Jonathan Gabe (eds), *Sociological Perspectives on the New Genetics* (Oxford: Blackwell, 1999), pp. 171–90.

14. Troy Duster, *Backdoor to Eugenics* (London: Routledge, 1990).

15. Mary Briody Mahowald, *Genes, Women, Equality* (New York: Oxford University Press, 2000), pp. 108–12.

16. T. Marteau and H. Drake, 'Attributions for Disability: The Influence of Genetic Screening', *Social Science and Medicine* 40 (1995), 1127–32.

17. On non-directiveness in genetic counselling, see Stella Reiter-Theil, 'Ethical Questions in Genetic Counselling: How Far Do Concepts Like "Non-Directivity" and "Ethical Neutrality" Help in Solving Problems?', in Maureen Junker-Kenny and Lisa Sowle Cahill (eds), *The Ethics of Genetic Engineering*, Concilium 1998/2 (London: SCM, and Maryknoll, NY: Orbis, 1998), pp. 23–34.

18. Quoted in *Genes Are Us? Attitudes to Genetics and Disability: A RADAR Survey.*

19. Cf. Paul, *Controlling Human Heredity*, pp. 134–5.

20. See further Troy Duster, 'Persistence and Continuity in Human Genetics and Social Stratification', in Ted Peters (ed.), *Genetics: Issues of Social Justice* (Cleveland, Ohio: Pilgrim Press, 1998), pp. 218–38; and Nelkin and Lindee, *DNA Mystique*, pp. 169–91.

21. Shakespeare, 'Choices and Rights: Eugenics, Genetics and Disability Equality', *Disability and Society* 13 (1998), 665–81 at 669.

22. Cf. Adrienne Asch, 'Prenatal Diagnosis and Selective Abortion: A Challenge to Practice and Policy', *American Journal of Public Health* 89 (1999), 1649–57, at 1652.

23. Karl Rahner, 'The Experiment with Man: Theological Observations on Man's Self-Manipulation', in *Theological Investigations* vol. IX (London: Darton, Longman and Todd, 1972), pp. 205–24, at 207.

24. Immune-system enhancements are discussed by LeRoy Walters and Julie Gage Palmer, *The Ethics of Gene Therapy* (New York: Oxford University Press, 1997), pp. 110–11.

25. John Harris, *Clones, Genes and Immortality* (Oxford: Oxford University Press, 1998), p. 191.

26. Ibid., p. 203.

27. Ibid., p. 194.

28. See in general Gerald McKenny, *To Relieve the Human Condition: Bioethics, Technology, and the Body* (Albany, NY: State University of New York Press), pp. 180–81.

29. The priority of care over cure is a prominent feature of Stanley Hauerwas's writings on medical ethics. See, for example, *Suffering Presence: Theological Reflections on Medicine, the Mentally Handicapped, and the Church* (Edinburgh: T. & T. Clark, 1986).

30. Cf. Shakespeare, 'Choices and Rights', 669–71.

31. Isaiah 53:2–3. For a valuable reflection on fragility, see Erik Parens, 'The Goodness of Fragility: On the Prospect of Genetic Technologies Aimed at the Enhancement of Human Capacities', *Kennedy Institute of Ethics Journal* 5 (1995), 141–53.

32. On the resurrection as the key to Christian belief in body–soul unity, see Oliver O'Donovan, 'Keeping Body and Soul Together', in Stephen E.

Lammers and Allen Verhey (eds), *On Moral Medicine: Theological Perspectives in Medical Ethics*, 2nd edn (Grand Rapids, Mi.: Eerdmans, 1998), pp. 223–38, esp. 228–31.

33. See Paul Ramsey, 'The Indignity of "Death with Dignity" ', in Lammers and Verhey (eds), *On Moral Medicine*, pp. 209–22.

34. David B. Biebel, 'The Riddle of Suffering', in John F. Kilner, Rebecca D. Pentz, and Frank E. Young (eds), *Genetic Ethics: Do the Ends Justify the Genes?* (Carlisle: Paternoster, and Grand Rapids, Mi.: Eerdmans, 1997), p. 3.

35. The relation between attitudes to human limits and different approaches to morality is discussed in Robert Song, 'Wisdom as the End of Morality', in Stephen Barton (ed.), *Where Shall Wisdom Be Found?* (Edinburgh: T. & T. Clark, 1999) pp. 295–306.

36. On a positive Christian appropriation of suffering, see McKenny, *To Relieve the Human Condition*, pp. 219–26.

37. See, for example, Norman Daniels, 'The Genome Project, Individual Differences, and Just Health Care', in Murphy and Lappé (eds), *Justice and the Human Genome Project*, pp. 110–32.

38. Eric T. Juengst, 'Can Enhancement Be Distinguished from Prevention in Genetic Medicine?', *Journal of Medicine and Philosophy* 22 (1997), 125–42. A fuller list of problems with the 'normal function' model is given by Erik Parens, 'Is Better Always Good? The Enhancement Project', in Erik Parens (ed.), *Enhancing Human Traits: Ethical and Social Implications* (Washington, DC: Georgetown University Press, 1998), pp. 1–28 at 5–10.

39. Juengst, 'Can Enhancement Be Distinguished from Prevention?', 139.

40. James C. Peterson, 'Ethical Standards for Genetic Intervention', in Kilner, Pentz and Young (eds), *Genetic Ethics*, pp. 193–202.

41. For other reasons for being dubious about correction for height, see Dónal P. O'Mathúna, 'The Case of Human Growth Hormone', in Kilner, Pentz and Young (eds), *Genetic Ethics*, pp. 203–17.

Chapter 4: **Justice, Community and Genetics**

1. See Robert Plomin, *The Psychologist* 14, no. 3 (March 2001), 135. That not all of the identical twins had autistic twins is of course also evidence of the environmental contribution to autism.

2. Plomin et al., *Behavioral Genetics* (New York: Freeman, 3rd edn, 1997), p. 220.

3. Richard J. Herrnstein and Charles Murray, *The Bell Curve: Intelligence and Class Structure in American Life* (New York: Free Press, 1994).

4. Alan R. Templeton, 'The Complexity of the Genotype-Phenotype Relationship and the Limitations of Using Genetic "Markers" at the Individual Level', *Science in Society* 11 (1998), 373–89.

5. Andrew Wilkie, 'How Will We Actually Use This Map to Find Our Way?', *The Psychologist* 14, no. 3 (March 2001), 150–51.

6. Indeed, what defines something as a genetic disease depends on what assumptions we make about the environment. As Steve Jones notes, if everyone smoked, lung cancer would be a genetic disease (*The Language of the Genes* (London: HarperCollins, 2nd edn, 2000), p. 103).

7. It is also worth noting a kind of 'paradox of heritability'. Because heritability is defined in terms of the proportion of phenotypic variance in a population which is due to genetic difference, a trait which is very largely genetically determined (e.g. having two eyes) may have a relatively low heritability, since a very high percentage of cases of deviation from this will be due to lifetime accidents. Societies which practise the *lex talionis* ('an eye for an eye') will have even lower heritabilities for two-eyedness than those that do not.

8. Joseph S. Alper and Jonathan Beckwith, 'Genetic Fatalism and Social Policy: The Implications of Behavior Genetics Research', *Yale Journal of Biology and Medicine* 65 (1993), 511–24 at 518.

9. Many such critics also erroneously assume that if something is caused by environmental rather than genetic factors, it is therefore readily malleable and in the realm of freedom.

10. See, in a US context, Robert J. Pokorski, 'Use of Genetic Information by Private Insurers', in Timothy F. Murphy and Marc A. Lappé (eds), *Justice and the Human Genome Project* (Berkeley: University of California Press, 1994), pp. 91–109.

11. This third approach is the one currently being adopted by the UK. In 1997 the Human Genetics Advisory Commission (HGAC) concluded that 'a requirement to disclose results of specific genetic tests ... would only be acceptable when a quantifiable association between a given pattern of test results and events actuarially relevant for a specific insurance product had been established' (*The Implications of Genetic Testing for Insurance*, para. 4.8). The government subsequently established an advisory committee, the Genetics and Insurance Committee (GAIC), which includes representatives of the insurance industry, whose function has been to assess the reliability of genetic tests for actuarial purposes. At the time of writing it had approved a test for Huntington's disease, and was considering some others.

12. Quoting one survey which argued that the additional costs would be nearer 10 per cent than 100 per cent, the HGAC report concluded that 'the life insurance industry could currently withstand limited adverse selection that might occur as a result of non-disclosure of genetic test results for life insurance' (para. 3.5).

13. Indeed, it is questionable how useful family histories are for insurance, given inevitable problems of vague medical descriptions and outright misdiagnosis, misattributed paternity, and so on.

14. Cf. in general Norman Daniels, 'The Genome Project, Individual Differences, and Just Health Care', in Murphy and Lappé (eds), *Justice and the Human Genome Project*, pp. 110–32, which includes a good moral discussion of standard underwriting practices.

15. See Mark Sagoff, 'DNA Patents: Making Ends Meet', in Audrey R. Chapman (ed.), *Perspectives on Genetic Patenting: Religion, Science and Industry in Dialogue* (Washington, DC: American Association for the Advancement of Science, 1999), pp. 245–67.

16. See further Pilar Ossario, 'Common Heritage Arguments against Patenting Human DNA', in Chapman (ed.), *Perspectives on Human Patenting*, pp. 89–108.

17. I owe these figures to Sol Benatar.

Chapter 5: **Technological Inevitability and Alternative Futures**

1. Lee Silver, *Remaking Eden: Cloning and Beyond in a Brave New World* (London: Weidenfeld and Nicolson, 1998), pp. 240–44.

2. Gerald McKenny, *To Relieve the Human Condition: Bioethics, Technology and the Body* (Albany, NY: State University of New York Press, 1997).

3. Ibid., p. 20.

4. On genetic essentialism in general, see Dorothy Nelkin and M. Susan Lindee, *The DNA Mystique: The Gene as a Cultural Icon* (New York: W. H. Freeman, 1995).

5. I have discussed the relation of the church to the public realm in *Christianity and Liberal Society* (Oxford: Clarendon Press, 1997), esp. the final chapter.

Glossary

In addition to the glossary of scientific terms, I have also given an extremely brief introduction to the science of genetics which contains all the basic ideas that you need to know in order to understand this book. Further reading is given in the Select Annotated Bibliography.

Genetics: a brief introduction to the science

There are about 100 trillion (i.e. about 100 million million) cells in the human body. These cells vary enormously in shape and size, depending on their function: nerve cells (neurons) are long and thin, for example, while skin cells are flat and wide. Within each cell there is a nucleus, which contains long string-like bodies known as chromosomes. In the case of human beings, there are 46 chromosomes in each cell nucleus, and these form two complete and more or less matching sets of the human genome. Each pair in the set is numbered from 1 to 22 in decreasing order of length, leaving two sex chromosomes which amongst other things determine the sex of the person (everybody has an X chromosome, but men also have a Y chromosome, while women have an additional X chromosome).

Chromosomes are made out of the molecule deoxyribonucleic acid (DNA). The structure of DNA is the familiar double helix, resembling a coiled rope ladder, which was first discovered by James Watson and Francis Crick in their Nobel-prize-winning work of 1953. Each of the rungs of the ladder is known as a base pair, since it links two bases or chemicals. These bases are of four kinds, adenine, cytosine, guanine, and thymine (often abbreviated as A, C, G, T), and each of the two strands of the double helix is comprised of extremely long chains of these four bases. They have the special property that each type of base only ever pairs up with one other: A always pairs up with T, and C with G. This means that each strand is a kind of mirror image of the other, a feature which enables the identical replication of DNA and is thus central to the copying mechanism of genetic material.

There are about three billion base pairs in the human genome, spread across the 23 chromosomes. The vast majority of this DNA, about 95 per cent, appears to serve no purpose and for this reason is known as 'junk DNA'. Stretched out amidst this sea of non-functional DNA, however, there are sequences which are clearly functional. Ranging from a few thousand to tens of millions of base pairs, these working sequences are known as genes; at latest estimates there are about 30,000 of them in the human genome. Genes provide the information which through complex processes known as transcription and translation allows cells to produce sequences of amino acids, which when completed and folded up are known as proteins. These proteins are the basic building blocks of the entire body.

Genetic engineering works by direct manipulation of DNA. Stretches of DNA can be cut up by special chemical scissors known as restriction enzymes and then connected to other bits of DNA. This process can be used to 'cut and paste' anything from a single base pair to a whole gene or more, generating recombinant DNA, and has been practised for many decades. It has been used to create transgenic bacteria, viruses, plants and animals, and could in principle be used in human sperm, eggs or embryos that would then be implanted in the womb. However, in human beings at any later stage than that of the embryo the problem of direct gene manipulation becomes acute: current gene therapy techniques, for example, turn not on direct replacement of defective genes through gene 'surgery', but on adding non-defective genes into a random place on the genome which it is hoped will safely express the correct protein.

The nature of heredity turns on another aspect of genetics. When ordinary body cells divide, a process known as mitosis, each chromosome forms an exact copy of itself, so that each of the daughter cells has a full complement of 46 chromosomes. However, to form eggs and sperm a specialised cell division known as meiosis occurs: here each pair of chromosomes lines up together and creates a single chromosome made up of genes in the same order as each of the parent chromosomes, but randomly chosen between them. This means that each sperm or egg cell has only 23 chromosomes, but that as a result of the random shuffling process, each has a unique set of genes. When the egg is fertilised, the two sets of chromosomes are united to form the full complement of 46, and the process of ordinary cell division continues until a new child comes into being.

Whenever cell division occurs, there is inevitably a minuscule chance of a mistake being made in the gene copying process. Such mistakes are known as mutations. They are not as such harmful: indeed they are the basis of all genetic variation, and in orthodox Darwinian theory are necessary for any process of evolution to occur at all. The process of mutation means that for each gene there are different – and often many different – versions (or alleles, as they are known). Each pair of genes in a particular person may therefore be the same, but they may also be different. Whether a change in a gene leads to a physical change depends on whether it is dominant or recessive: this feature, along with many of the basic ideas of the scientific study of heredity, was first discovered in the 1850s and 1860s by the Austrian monk Gregor Mendel working on pea plants in his monastery gardens.

It can be illustrated by reference to alleles which happen to cause diseases. In the case of recessive diseases, both alleles need to be faulty for the disease to occur: a person who has only one faulty allele will be a carrier of the disease but will not typically suffer from it. Examples of such recessive diseases are cystic fibrosis, Tay-Sachs disease and thalassaemia. Dominant disorders such as Huntington's disease, by contrast, will occur even if the individual has only one faulty copy of the gene. Dominant disorders are usually seen in several generations of a family, whilst there is usually no previous family history in the case of recessive diseases. On average one in twenty-five white Europeans or North Americans is a carrier of a fault in the gene for cystic fibrosis, which means that in about one in 625 couples both will be carriers; of their children, on average two out of four will be carriers but will not suffer the disease, one in four will have the disease, and one in four will neither suffer the disease nor be a carrier.

Glossary of scientific terms

Allele: there can be a number of different versions of each gene; each version is called an allele.

Base pair: the linked pair of chemical bases that forms each 'rung' of the DNA double helix; there are about three billion in the human genome. A base is also known as a nucleotide.

Behavioural genetics: the study of the genetic influence on individual behaviour. See also quantitative genetics.

Chromosome: a long filament-like string consisting of DNA and supporting proteins, along which genes are found. There are 46 chromosomes in a human cell arranged in pairs: 22 pairs of autosomes, and 2 sex chromosomes.

Cloning: the technique of producing a genetically identical cell through the insertion of the genetic material from the nucleus of an adult cell into an egg cell from which the chromosomes have been removed. Cloning is also used in a more general sense to refer to all insertion of recombinant DNA into a bacterium, for the purposes of creating more DNA and the like. See also reproductive cloning and therapeutic cloning.

DNA: deoxyribonucleic acid, the molecule which encodes genetic information.

DNA chips: micro-arrays which can test for hundreds of genes simultaneously.

Dominant disorder: a disorder which occurs even if only one copy of the two matching genes is faulty. Compare recessive disorder.

Embryo screening: screening of embryos for defects (including chromosomal disorders), determination of sex, or suitability for implantation in the womb. PGD is one form of embryo screening.

Environment: in relation to genetics, the contributory factor to an organism's phenotype that is not due to its genotype; as such it includes not only external, non-biological influences, but also biological influences such as those a fetus experiences in the womb.

Gene: a functional sequence of DNA which codes for a protein. There are currently thought to be about 30,000 genes in the human genome.

Gene sequencing: reading the order of individual bases of a gene.

Gene therapy: a therapeutic technique which uses recombinant DNA technology to replace a disease gene or to insert a healthy version of a gene into a cell nucleus.

Genetic enhancement: a technique which uses recombinant DNA technology to enhance the characteristics of an organism.

Genetic marker: a readily identifiable sequence on a chromosome. In some cases genetic markers can be used to signpost the probable location of a particular gene.

Genome: the full complement of DNA contained by an organism.

Genotype: the genetic constitution of an organism. Compare phenotype.

Germ-line gene therapy: a form of gene therapy which is targeted at sperm, eggs, or early embryos, such that the therapy would be of benefit not only to the individual but also to all their descendants. Compare somatic-cell gene therapy.

Heritability: the measure of genetic influence on a trait. It is strictly defined as the variance of a trait in a population due to genetic differences divided by the total variance of the trait in that population, and is always defined for a particular population and for a particular environment.

Human Genome Project: the international project launched in 1990 to sequence and map the entire human genome.

In vitro **fertilisation (IVF)**: a technique for fertilising an egg outside a woman's body.

Multifactorial: a multifactorial trait or disorder is one that is influenced by both genetic and environmental factors. Compare polygenic and single-gene traits.

PGD (pre-implantation genetic diagnosis): the laboratory examination of embryos to diagnose potential genetic disorders before possible implantation in the womb.

Pharmacogenomics (or pharmacogenetics): the science of tailoring drugs to suit the genetic make-up of individuals.

Phenotype: the observable constitution of an organism.

Polygenic: a polygenic trait or disorder is one that is determined by more than one gene. Compare single-gene and multifactorial traits.

Protein: a molecule which forms the basic building block of a living organism; proteins are comprised of chains of amino acids, strung together in an order specified by the sequence of base pairs in a gene.

Recessive disorder: a disorder which occurs only when both copies of the two matching genes are faulty. Compare dominant disorder.

Recombinant DNA technology: techniques which cut and splice DNA in order to create new DNA sequences.

Reproductive cloning: the use of cloning techniques with a view to creating a cloned child; also known as full-pregnancy cloning. Contrast therapeutic cloning.

Single-gene trait or disorder: a trait or disorder that is attributable to a single gene – for example, Huntington's disease or cystic fibrosis. Compare multifactorial and polygenic traits.

Somatic cell: any cell in the body except for sperm or eggs.

Somatic-cell gene therapy: a form of gene therapy targeted at the somatic cells (e.g. lungs, liver, skin) of an individual.

Stem cells: cells from which cells of a tissue type are derived. Embryonic stem cells are totipotent – that is, capable of being turned into any type of cell in the body.

Therapeutic cloning: the use of cloning techniques to create embryos which will not be implanted in the womb but cultivated for other therapeutic uses, especially through stem-cell techniques. Contrast reproductive cloning.

X-linked disorder: a disorder for which the gene is on the X chromosome; therefore typically affects only males, since they have only one copy of the X chromosome. Examples include Duchenne muscular dystrophy and some forms of colour-blindness.

Select Annotated Bibliography

The science of human genetics

For those who wish to understand the scientific aspects of genetics further whilst still remaining at the level of popular science, both of the following introductions are commended: Steve Jones, *The Language of the Genes* (London: HarperCollins, 2nd edn, 2000), and Matt Ridley, *Genome: The Autobiography of a Species in 23 Chapters* (London: Fourth Estate, 1999). At a serious undergraduate textbook level, see, for example, Robert F. Mueller and Ian D. Young, *Emery's Elements of Medical Genetics* (Edinburgh Churchill Livingstone, 11th edn, 2001). Excellent, up-to-date accounts of recent developments can be found weekly in *New Scientist* and monthly in *Scientific American*.

Theological approaches

Good short theological introductions to bioethics as a whole are found in Gilbert Meilaender, *Bioethics: A Primer for Christians* (Grand Rapids, Mi.: Eerdmans, 1996) (Protestant), and Helen Watt, *Life and Death in Healthcare Ethics: A Short Introduction* (London: Routledge, 2000) (Roman Catholic). An outstanding and comprehensive anthology of Christian theological approaches to every area of bioethics, containing over a thousand pages of readings, is Stephen E. Lammers and Allen Verhey, *On Moral Medicine: Theological Perspectives in Medical Ethics* (Grand Rapids, Mi.: Eerdmans, 2nd edn, 1998). Neil Messer, (ed.), *Theological Issues in Bioethics: An Introduction with Readings* (London: Darton, Longman and Todd, 2002) is also strongly recommended.

Some of the most significant theological discussions of genetic issues were held a generation ago. Amongst prominent contributors were the Protestant Paul Ramsey (e.g. *Fabricated Man: The Ethics of Genetic Control* (New Haven: Yale University Press, 1970)), the situation ethicist Joseph Fletcher (e.g. *The Ethics of Genetic Control: Ending Reproductive Roulette* (Garden City, NY: Anchor, 1974)), and the Roman Catholic Richard McCormick (see essays collected in *How Brave A New World? Dilemmas in Bioethics* (London: SCM Press, 1981)). One of the single best books published on a Christian approach to bioethics in recent years, which has been very influential on much of my approach, is Gerald McKenny, *To Relieve the Human Condition: Bioethics, Technology, and the Body* (Albany, NY: State University of New York Press, 1997); note that it is not an introductory book. Helpful collections of essays on Christian approaches to genetics include John F. Kilner, Rebecca D. Pentz, and Frank E. Young (eds), *Genetic Ethics: Do the Ends Justify the Genes?* (Carlisle: Paternoster, and Grand Rapids, Mi.: Eerdmans, 1997), and Maureen Junker-Kenny and Lisa Sowle Cahill (eds), *The Ethics of Genetic Engineering*, Concilium 1998/2 (London: SCM, and Maryknoll, NY: Orbis, 1998). Audrey R. Chapman, *Unprecedented Choices: Religious Ethics at the Frontier of Genetic Science* (Minneapolis: Fortress, 1999) includes a very useful historical overview of responses to the new genetics both by denominational bodies and by individual theologians and ethicists. Other recent theological contributions have included works by Ted Peters (e.g.

Playing God? Genetic Determinism and Human Freedom (New York: Routledge, 1997)), and Ronald Cole-Turner (e.g. *The New Genesis: Theology and the Genetic Revolution* (Louisville, Ky.: Westminster John Knox Press, 1993)).

For theological work on genetics in plants and animals, see Donald Bruce and Ann Bruce (eds), *Engineering Genesis: The Ethics of Genetic Engineering in Non-Human Species* (London: Earthscan, 1998).

Chapter 1: **Introduction**
On genetics and popular culture, both Dorothy Nelkin and Susan Lindee, *The DNA Mystique: The Gene as Cultural Icon* (New York: W. H. Freeman, 1995) and Jon Turney, *Frankenstein's Footsteps: Science, Genetics and Popular Culture* (New Haven: Yale University Press, 1998) are highly recommended.

Chapter 2: **Health, Medicine and the New Genetics**
The Human Genome Project and some of its implications is covered in Daniel J. Kevles and LeRoy Hood (eds), *The Code of Codes: Scientific and Social Issues in the Human Genome Project* (Cambridge, Ma.: Harvard University Press, 1992), though inevitably some of this is dated; and Philip R. Sloan (ed.), *Controlling Our Destinies: Historical, Philosophical, Ethical and Theological Perspectives on the Human Genome Project* (Notre Dame, Ind.: University of Notre Dame Press, 2000).

Alice Wexler, *Mapping Fate: A Memoir of Family, Risk and Genetic Research* (New York: Random House, 1995) is a moving, partly autobiographical account of the story of the search for the gene for Huntington's disease, by someone herself affected, while Charles R. Bosk, *All God's Mistakes: Genetic Counselling in a Pediatric Hospital* (Chicago: University of Chicago Press, 1992) is an account of a sociologist's encounter with the reality of genetic disease in children.

On gene therapy, see LeRoy Walters and Julie Gage Palmer, *The Ethics of Human Gene Therapy* (New York: Oxford University Press, 1997). On cloning, a good reader is Gregory E. Pence (ed.), *Flesh of My Flesh: The Ethics of Cloning Humans* (Lanham, Md.: Rowman & Littlefield, 1998), while Ronald Cole-Turner (ed.), *Human Cloning: Religious Responses* (Louisville, Ky.: Westminster John Knox Press, 1997) gives a range of Christian responses. Gregory Pence's *Who's Afraid of Human Cloning?* (Lanham, Md.: Rowman & Littlefield, 1998) is worth mentioning, even if only as a case study of how *not* to do bioethics.

A helpful practical guide to ethical issues connected to genetic testing and screening, which are not extensively covered in this book, is found in British Medical Association, *Human Genetics: Choice and Responsibility* (Oxford: Oxford University Press, 1998).

Chapter 3: **Genetic Enhancement and the New Eugenics**
The standard history of eugenics is Daniel Kevles, *In the Name of Eugenics: Genetics and the Uses of Human Heredity* (Cambridge, Ma.: Harvard University Press, 2nd edn, 1995). A good overview of the sociological and psychological dimensions of the new genetics is Theresa Marteau and Martin Richards (eds), *The Troubled Helix: Social and Psychological Implications of the New Human Genetics* (Cambridge: Cambridge University Press, 1996).

Tom Shakespeare (ed.), *The Disability Reader* (London: Continuum, 1998) is a highly recommended introduction to issues connected with disability.

A very good text on therapy and enhancement issues is Erik Parens (ed.), *Enhancing Human Traits: Ethical and Social Implications* (Washington, DC: Georgetown University Press, 1998). Many of the theological books listed above also touch on the theme.

Chapter 4: **Justice, Community and Genetics**

Issues of justice and genetics are covered in Timothy F. Murphy and Marc A. Lappé (eds), *Justice and the Human Genome Project* (Berkeley: University of California Press, 1994); Ted Peters (ed.), *Genetics: Issues of Social Justice* (Cleveland, Ohio: Pilgrim Press, 1998); and Allen Buchanan, Dan W. Brock, Norman Daniels, and Daniel Wikler, *From Chance to Choice: Genetics and Justice* (Cambridge: Cambridge University Press, 2000). For the global context, see Solomon R. Benatar, 'A Perspective from Africa on Human Rights and Genetic Engineering', in Justine Burley (ed.), *The Genetic Revolution and Human Rights* (Oxford: Oxford University Press, 1999), pp. 159–89. A feminist approach to genetics is Mary Briody Mahowald, *Genes, Women, Equality* (New York: Oxford University Press, 2000).

A standard but very readable textbook introduction to behavioural genetics is Robert Plomin, J. C. Defries, Gerald E. McClearn and Peter McGuffin, *Behavioral Genetics* (New York: W. H. Freeman, 4th edn, 2000). For an alternative view on some of the issues see Steven Rose, *Lifelines: Biology, Determinism, Freedom* (London: Penguin, 2nd edn, 1998). Probably the single most controverted area of behavioural genetics has been intelligence. For an introduction to the issues with a good bibliography, see Ian J. Deary, *Intelligence: A Very Short Introduction* (Oxford: Oxford University Press, 2001); for scepticism about the notions of intelligence and intelligence testing, see Ken Richardson, *The Making of Intelligence* (London: Weidenfeld and Nicolson, 1999), and Stephen Jay Gould's highly entertaining *The Mismeasure of Man* (London: Penguin, 2nd edn, 1997).

Patenting issues, particularly in relation to religious ethics, are well covered in Audrey R. Chapman (ed.), *Perspectives on Genetic Patenting: Religion, Science and Industry in Dialogue* (Washington, DC: American Association for the Advancement of Science, 1999).

There is no obvious published source to turn to first on genetics and insurance, but the website of the Genetics and Insurance Research Centre at Heriot-Watt University, Edinburgh, is a good place to start: *http://www.ma.hw.ac.uk/ams/res/girc.html*.

Further reading

For those wishing to read further in the theological ethics of genetics or other related bioethical fields, Lammers and Verhey (cited above) is recommended for its bibliographies. The standard multi-volume work on bioethics, with extensive bibliographical referencing, is Warren T. Reich (ed.), *Encyclopedia of Bioethics*, 5 vols. (New York: Macmillan, 2nd edn, 1995).

Inevitably much detailed work is published in journals. Christian journals on bioethics include *Christian Bioethics* and *Ethics and Medicine*, though much is also published in other journals devoted to theology (such as *Theological Studies* or *Religious Studies Review*) or Christian ethics (for example, *Studies in Christian Ethics* or *Journal of Religious Ethics*). There are many philosophical journals devoted to bioethics: amongst them *Hastings Center Report* (probably the premier journal in the field), *Journal of Medical Ethics*, *Journal of Medicine and Philosophy*, and *Bioethics*.

The number of websites devoted to bioethics is legion, as a casual visit to a search engine will demonstrate, but especially helpful are the Centre for Bioethics and Human Dignity's website (*http://www.cbhd.org*), which contains a daily bioethics news update and other on-line resources, and the National Reference Center for Bioethics Literature at Georgetown University (*http://www.georgetown.edu/research/nrcbl/*), which has links to extensive bioethics bibliographical databases.

Index